IRRIGATION DITCH, FORT ROMIE.

IRRIGATION FLUME, FORT ROMIE.

THE
POOR AND THE LAND

MORE WILDSIDE CLASSICS

THE
POOR AND THE LAND

BEING A REPORT ON THE

SALVATION ARMY COLONIES

IN THE UNITED STATES AND AT
HADLEIGH, ENGLAND

WITH

SCHEME OF
NATIONAL LAND SETTLEMENT

AND AN INTRODUCTION

by

H. RIDER HAGGARD

WILDSIDE PRESS

FIRST PUBLISHED IN 1905

THE POOR AND THE LAND

This edition published in 2007 by Wildside Press, LLC.
www.wildsidepress.com

This is America—a town of a few thousand, in a region of wheat and corn and dairies and little groves.

The town is, in our tale, called "Gopher Prairie, Minnesota." But its Main Street is the continuation of Main Streets everywhere. The story would be the same in Ohio or Montana, in Kansas or Kentucky or Illinois, and not very differently would it be told Up York State or in the Carolina hills.

Main Street is the climax of civilization. That this Ford car might stand in front of the Bon Ton Store, Hannibal invaded Rome and Erasmus wrote in Oxford cloisters. What Ole Jenson the grocer says to Ezra Stowbody the banker is the new law for London, Prague, and the unprofitable isles of the sea; whatsoever Ezra does not know and sanction, that thing is heresy, worthless for knowing and wicked to consider.

Our railway station is the final aspiration of architecture. Sam Clark's annual hardware turnover is the envy of the four counties which constitute God's Country. In the sensitive art of the Rosebud Movie Palace there is a Message, and humor strictly moral.

Such is our comfortable tradition and sure faith. Would he not betray himself an alien cynic who should otherwise portray Main Street, or distress the citizens by speculating whether there may not be other faiths?

INTRODUCTION

BLUE-BOOKS never have been and probably never will be a popular branch of literature. However difficult it may be, indeed, to collect the material and to write a treatise of this nature, it is undoubtedly far more difficult to persuade any one to study the same when written. Whether it is the colour that repels, or the size, or the big, closely printed page, the fact remains that no one reads a blue-book unless he is absolutely compelled so to do, and then not infrequently he contents himself with the Synopsis of Documents at the beginning and, perhaps, the concluding paragraphs. Moreover not one person in ten thousand is aware that such works, like others, can be purchased through any bookseller, that is by ordering them, since they are not usually kept in stock.

These, with the hope that thus it may reach a wider public, are the considerations, and not any expectation of gain, that have induced the author and, I may add, the publishers of the following pages to seek the kind permission of His Majesty's Treasury and of the Rhodes Trustees to re-issue [Cd. 2562] in its present form.

The original and official title of [Cd. 2562] is "Report on the Salvation Army Colonies in the United States and at Hadleigh, England, with Scheme of National Land Settlement, by Commissioner H. Rider Haggard". This Report with its annexed documents was presented

v

to both Houses of Parliament by command of His Majesty in June, 1905, and has now, I read, been referred to the consideration of a Departmental Committee.

Perhaps it will be as well to begin this Fore-word or Introduction with a very brief summary of the Report itself in the hope that the reader may be sufficiently interested thereby to be induced to attempt the effort of a more intimate acquaintance with its substance.

In February of the present year, on the initiative of the Rhodes Trustees who contributed a sum of money to meet expenses, I was nominated a Commissioner by the Secretary of State for the Colonies and despatched to the United States for the purpose of inspecting three land settlements which have been established in that country by the charitable and social Organisation known as the Salvation Army, *viz.*, in California, not very far from San Francisco, in Colorado, and in Ohio respectively. The object of this investigation is very clearly set out in the second paragraph of my letter of commission, which runs :—

" It appears to the Secretary of State that, if these experiments are found to be successful, some analogous system might, with great advantage, be applied in transferring the urban populations of the United Kingdom to different parts of the British Empire ".

Further, I was authorised, in the event of the experiments by the Salvation Army recommending themselves to me, to include in my report any practical suggestions that might occur to me, as to the means and methods whereby the example can best be turned to use in connection with the projected transfer of urban populations of the United Kingdom to different parts of the British Empire.

I will now sum up the results of this Mission and recapitulate in few words the recommendations and suggestions which I have ventured to offer to His Majesty's Government.

I was on the whole extremely well satisfied with the Californian and Colorado Settlements which are named Fort Romie and Fort Amity. Fort Herrick in Ohio, which I visited also, may be left out of the account, inasmuch as it is in the main devoted to the redemption of inebriates and to the carrying out of certain agricultural experiments. At both Fort Romie and Fort Amity, as may be seen by my Remarks on those places, I found the settlers healthy, happy, hopeful, and, almost without exception, doing well. Beginning in nearly every case with nothing, moreover, in the course of about four years at Fort Romie these settlers are now worth an average of over £400 per head above all their debts and liabilities to the Salvation Army and others, and at Fort Amity an average of over £200, which is, needless to say, a great deal more than they could possibly have accumulated during the same period as day-labourers on the land or in the cities.

The venture, however, has not proved so prosperous to its founders, the Salvation Army, who on these two settlements have incurred a total loss of about £10,000. This loss, not very large it is true, although quite as much as any charitable Body can wish to face, is due to four causes: (1) The facts that the Settlements were established by aid of money borrowed at a heavy rate of interest, namely 5 and 6 per cent., and that the settlers were charged too little for their holdings which they pay for by instalments. (2) The considerable initial cost of the estate both at Fort Romie and Fort Amity. (3) The fact that the settlers were first established at Fort Romie before the soil had been properly irrigated and at once confronted by a three years' drought. (4) The circumstance that at Fort Amity the land, which was virgin prairie, proved exceptionally hard to work; also to be impregnated with alkali or natural salts, whereof the presence was totally unsuspected at the time of buying, of which alkali it has cost much money to be rid by deep-draining.

So it comes about that although the settlers are doing so well, the Salvation Army have been called upon to pay £10,000 for their experience. My own view is that under all the circumstances and in face of the principles demonstrated and the success won in every other direction, this has been very cheaply bought. Further, I cannot see any cause to fear a repetition of that loss in the future application of those principles. It is therefore totally inaccurate to say, as has been done widely in press summaries of my report, that these Settlements are "financially a failure".

Indeed if the Settlements are carried out on the lines which I suggest, and especially if they are located upon good land which has cost the controlling Authority nothing, there should be, as is indicated by the tables that I have furnished, no loss but a considerable gain. Here I may state that this opportunity has arisen, since I was sufficiently successful in convincing the Government of the Dominion of Canada of the soundness and practicability of my scheme to induce them to make a formal offer of 360 square miles of territory to enable it to be put into operation as a beginning, with the promise, should it prove successful, of as much more land as may be required. This means that a huge estate of some of the best land in America, worth, even in its undeveloped condition, a great sum of money, is lying there waiting our good pleasure to occupy it and turn its emptiness to wealth.

As for the scheme itself it is so simple that I can only wonder no one has propounded it before. Also I believe that whenever it is put to work, as soon or late must certainly happen, it will be found very far-reaching in its effects. Here it is in a sentence : To combine a judicious use of the Public Credit with that of what I have called the "waste forces of Benevolence," and by means of these two levers to lift some of the mass of human misery which demonstrates itself in the great cities of civilisation to a new level of plenty and contentment.

There are those who urge, however, that all such efforts are misconceived and useless. Thus I will quote from a discussion of my scheme by an ably conducted provincial journal which I respect although I, who have no faith in the shibboleths of Party and am not of its bond-servants, do not always agree with certain of its judgments. It says : " No attempts to dispose of social wreckage in special ways will avail, so long as a defective social organisation is allowed to continue producing wreckage. The business of reformers is not to discover special methods of dealing with our social and industrial failures, but so to remedy the normal and ordinary condition of things as to cease producing a class that has to be watched and selected and labour colonised."

Counsels of perfection indeed and very well put ! But what do they come to ? That we must wait for something like a revolution followed by a millennium, for surely nothing short of these will produce so wondrous a change in our national conditions and thus prevent the production of "wreckage," that is of the destitute poor. But sudden and violent remedies are not in the way of an ancient people who prefer to glide "from precedent to precedent," also revolutions of whatever sort have not been observed to precede millenniums.

Such a doctrine seems to me indeed to violate all the laws of political or personal medicine. It is as though one said : These children are very ill, but some of them at any rate could be cured and become splendid citizens,

soldiers, farmers, wives and mothers. Do not, however,
attempt any such thing. Much as wholesome population may be needed, let them rot and die. Devote your
efforts to preventing unhealthy folk from marrying in
future, or if that is not feasible, ask them to be good
enough to have no diseased children, or, if necessary, as
a last resource, wait till a miracle occurs which makes
everybody healthy.

In answer to such arguments I can only say that,
being anxious that something should be done within
the next few generations, I am content to face things
as they are. I do not believe in any panacea that will
remedy their " normal and ordinary condition ". I do
not know what such a nostrum can be, or whence it
can come : I wish that I did. Was it not said of old
that the Poor are always with us ? But the Speaker
did not add that on this account we should abandon
as futile our attempts to help the Poor. In short, because we have neither the means nor the material to
build palaces of marble and set them to live therein in
riches, I do not think that we should therefore despise
warm, if humble dwellings of moulded clay that will
serve to shelter many a houseless one from the fury of
the storm and many a lost child from the cold and the
dangers of the night.

To return: that much benevolence is uselessly diffused,
losing itself in the sands of vain or ill-directed effort,
and that more runs to absolute waste, no one of experience will deny.

To give an illustration : With all this diverse flood of
unutilised kindness and brotherly love that yearns to
help but lacks the means or knows not how, I would
do what the electrical engineer does with a noble and
convenient torrent. Thus for unnumbered ages the
great Zambesi in Africa has thundered down its cliffs in
beautiful but useless foam, which, when it is harnessed,

will drive every engine within a thousand miles. The citizen of Pretoria or Johannesburg may never have seen the Zambesi Falls, yet those far-off Falls, that for all the past have been unserviceable to man, will one day be at work continually, stamping the ore in his mine, running the carriage in his street, lighting the lamp by his bed ; making life cleaner, cheaper, easier. Thus, I believe, it may be too with those waste forces of Benevolence whereof I speak, when by help of that machinery of the Public Credit they are applied to the salvation of the poor, and so dedicated to the welfare of the earth.

I think also most of my readers will agree with me that, notwithstanding the all-prevalent evil which in a thousand shapes haunts the footsteps of our race, Good is still the mightiest power in the world, and, if its aimless strength could be concentrated and directed, would go far towards effecting a reformation of the world. This is a large proposition, but, to confine it to the matter in hand, under these circumstances that power of charity which never faileth and covereth all things would certainly suffice to empty the sinks of our cities, to re-distribute population, to give to the starving that food which awaits them in such abundance on the bosom of the earth, to provide the slum-stifled child with pure air and space wherein to grow to a wholesome and unfettered maturity, and to replenish the nations with that vigour which the press and sorrow of the towns are sapping from their wearied blood.

The reader may ask how this combination of credit and charity is to be arranged. I answer thus : (1) Through the guarantee by the State of the interest on loans, for the repayment of which loans and interest the land to be settled should prove a sufficient security, since that land will be sold—not given—to the settlers and paid for by them in instalments. (2) By making use of any willing, approved and well-established charitable Body, Organisation or Society, to administer the loans and Settlements under proper Government authority and control. In this fashion the cost of local official direction, which would, I believe, prove almost fatal to the scheme as a business proposition, may be obviated, and that bond of human sympathy and kindness inspired by love and not by lucre imported into its working, which, in my view, is, in fact, necessary to its complete success.

Says one of my critics : " We cannot understand what Mr. Rider Haggard means when he says that the cost of adequate Imperial supervision would be prohibitive. Surely what the Salvation Army can do, the Government is also able to do ? "

If this writer had thought the matter out surely he would have understood. The proposal is to select suitable poor persons from the cities, to convey them to distant lands, establish them there, instruct them, live with them for thirty years in the various settlements, all of which, under my plan, will be done by charitable Bodies using highly trained and specialised men, at the price of their *out-of-pocket expenses only*. What would such men cost in the market, if, in any number, they are obtainable at all ? A large figure I imagine.

Moreover, if they can be obtained—*quis custodiet ipsos custodes ?*—who would or could look after them at the ends of the earth and be sure that they kept industrious, sober and honest, or did not waste, mismanage or oppress ? Philanthropic Organisations with their own credit at stake and representatives in every Colony alone have this in their power ; moreover, the servants of such Organisations in most cases are subject to a stricter master, namely, their own consciences.

The matter, however, could easily be put to proof. Let two colonial Settlements be organised, one on the lines of my Scheme and the other directed from London by the Imperial Government alone without assistance of any kind. Then let the results be tabulated and their cost compared. Indeed there is no vital principle involved in such an alteration of my plan. If the Nation or its Government wishes to reject all philanthropic assistance and to retain the selection of settlers and the subsequent management of the settlements entirely in its own hands, and is prepared to defray the extra cost, by all means make the experiment. Only then there is a danger that the Country may weary of paying the bill. Also the project that I had hoped to inaugurate is one of imperial investment, not of imperial charity.

Such is the scheme which I have submitted for consideration in this Report. Needless to say, if I may judge from what I have heard and the great number of press notices that I receive, already it has been widely criticised. Most of that criticism, so far as I am acquainted with it, is, I am proud to add, remarkably favourable in its character, while some of that which is unfavourable evidently has been founded, not upon the Report itself which the critic has found no opportunity of perusing, but upon a telegraphic summary whence many vital points and qualifications have been omitted. Still certain comments have been advanced adversely with which I will try to deal as best I can.

The first and chief of these, for with the principle of the State guaranteed loan secured upon the settler's land and repayable by instalments little or no fault seems to be found, at any rate in the press, is that my plan would amount to an " endowment " of the Salvation Army, or to the " subsidising of a voluntary Agency".

Variants of this objection are that the work should be carried out from start to finish by an Imperial Emigration Department only, which, as I demonstrate, could

only be done at a crushing expense; that the Salvation
Army is not to be trusted; that it would be unwise to
hand over the task to them; that there should be complete State control, even in the details of distant local
administration, and that the employment of the Salvation Army for this purpose might involve undue religious
pressure.

If we except the second head, namely, the proposal
that none except the Imperial Emigration Authority
should touch the matter, and the third, that of the
amount of confidence that may be given to the Salvation Army, which, after all, must remain a matter of
opinion, I can only suppose that the framers of these
arguments have not adequately studied the suggestions
made in my Report.

No endowment or subsidising of the Salvation Army
is therein proposed, nor is it proposed that they should
be exclusively employed in this business. The actual
words of my suggestion are "that the Salvation Army,
*or any other well-established and approved social, charitable
or religious Organisation*, should be deputed to carry out
the work of selecting, distributing and organising the
settlers on land-colonies anywhere within the boundaries
of the British Empire, who should remain in charge of
such Organisation until all liabilities were paid".

Thus, if they could pass certain necessary tests, it
would be open to any Corporation to take advantage
of this scheme in order to establish land-settlements
at home or abroad for the benefit of poor persons of
British origin.

For example, I observe that the Church Army propose to form certain colonies of this nature in England,
and are appealing, or are about to appeal, for subscriptions to aid them in their good work. If my scheme
were in operation they would be entitled to come to the
Superintendent of Land-Settlements and, after satis-

fying him and his superiors of their *bona fides* and the
feasibility of their proposal as a workable undertaking,
to claim a *per capita* grant upon the arranged terms in
order to enable them or to assist them to carry it out.
Again, it might help the Jewish community in the
matter of the Zionist Settlements for poor Hebrews,
which are so much discussed among them at the present time.   And so forth *ad infinitum.*

At present, however, the Salvation Army are in the
position of sole tenderers.   At least I am not aware
of the existence of any other Body of the sort that is
prepared, to whatever extent may be desired, to trans-
port persons from the cities to distant colonies and there
to take charge of them and instruct them over a long
period of years, receiving in return only actual out-of-
pocket expenses and the loan of the funds necessary
to the enterprise, or rather the authority, subject to
proper audit, to administer that loan upon particular
settlements.   When such Bodies arise and appear their
applications would doubtless receive fair and proper consideration.

Meanwhile it may be pointed out that the Salvation
Army have many qualifications for the work, inasmuch
as they are well established in almost every British
colony and already possess a large staff of trained officers
well fitted to direct agricultural settlements, which staff
they are willing to increase indefinitely.   Also they have
the advantage of the confidence of the Government of
Canada and, I believe, of that of other British colonies.
Indeed, although there are circumstances in his case
that might have been expected to incline him to a
different opinion, Sir Wilfrid Laurier, the Prime Minister of the Canadian Dominion, informed me expressly
at an official interview that he considered that there was
no Institution so well fitted to carry out such a scheme
as I had in my mind as were the Salvation Army.

b

Whether or no this Salvation Army can be trusted in other ways, as I have said, must remain a matter of opinion.

My own views thereon may be gathered from my Report, and certainly they enjoy to a remarkable degree the confidence of those classes that it is proposed to help; indeed countless numbers of the poor of all races throughout the world trust them entirely. This, I consider, is sufficiently demonstrated by the circumstance that during the present and last years (1904-1905) they have with remarkable success emigrated to Canada many settlers, I believe about five thousand. If, however, they should be proved to be untrustworthy, or should fail in the duties which they undertake, it must be remembered that the system of capitation grants is one that is easily controlled, as it is, in effect, a system of payment by results. Meanwhile I am content to obey an ancient precept and to judge the tree by its fruits.

To come to the question of the possibility of the exercise of undue religious pressure upon settlers or their children. If the reader will turn to my Remarks upon the Fort Romie Colony, he will see it stated there in paragraph 23 that I ascertained that the Salvation Army place no religious pressure upon the colonists and enforce no religious tests, moreover that among these colonists are members of the Roman Catholic and other faiths.

At Hadleigh also I found that on the Sunday previous to my visit the manager of the Colony had taken about a hundred of its inhabitants to attend the parish church. Further, in the Memorandum of Information drawn up by the Salvation Army respecting their colony at Fort Amity, it is stated expressly that " the Colony is not in any sense intended for Salvationists only; in fact the majority of the residents here are not members of the Organisation ". Lastly, I believe that I am right in saying that the Salvation Army are non-sectarian in their work, and that they shelter more than 20,000 persons daily in their refuges and institutions throughout the world, of which great number less than 5 per cent. are Salvationists.

Arguing from all these premises, therefore, I consider that it would be easy to over-rate the danger of any narrow or bigoted treatment by the Salvation Army of the colonists whom the State might entrust to their charge. Also provisions are inserted in the Report to guard against any such contingencies, and, as I have stated, the work need not, and, I trust, would not be confined to any single Society.

The second main objection is—and this I find in sundry places—that, if my scheme is put to work, without doubt it will take a great many people out of Britain. Evidently this is so, but I will premise my remarks upon the subject by pointing out that such emigration was what Mr. Secretary Lyttelton had in his mind when he directed me to report, as may be seen from paragraph 2 of his first letter of Commission to myself. I was therefore bound to confine myself to that side of the subject. I have, however, in paragraph 39 of my Report, anticipated this criticism with which I express myself in " great sympathy ". Indeed, to tell the truth, I have always considered this aspect of the question much more important than any other, as, I think, will be admitted by readers of my work, *Rural England*.

Also I have ventured, should I be so directed by His Majesty's Government, to offer to prepare a separate report upon the Home prospects of the matter, namely, as to whether it would or would not be possible to establish rural colonies in the United Kingdom. As I may possibly be ordered to investigate and express a formal opinion upon this business, the reader will understand that for the present, so far as it is concerned, my lips are closed. I will only add, therefore, that in this direction also I think that I can see glimmerings of light, but I should like to inspect the small holdings of Denmark, and, if possible, those of New Zealand, made under the Advances to Settlers Act, before expressing a final opinion.

It is, however, perhaps allowable to say generally, that the problem is quite different from that dealt with in these pages. That, if formed more or less upon the lines I have advanced, such settlements can be set up upon highly fertile land in Canada, given free of cost to the Home Government by that of the Dominion, or, under similar conditions, in other places in the British Empire, and pay their way, I am as sure as I can be of anything in this uncertain world. In the United Kingdom, however, the conditions are different. Here the land must be bought for no mean sum, and there are such things as Rates, Tithe and Taxes to be faced. Also that land would probably lie in the power of Rural District Councils, Bodies against whose decisions, however wrong and unreasonable they may be, there seems to exist no effective appeal, so that the cost of housing the settlers would be much greater than it is in Canada and other Colonies.

For these reasons and others which I need not enter into, it would be rash to assume that a report made by any competent and honest man who keeps before him the desirability of preventing such schemes from becoming a burden upon the tax-payer or the rates, would of necessity be of a favourable character. That it might be so, in common with thousands of others I earnestly hope, since after the very extensive investigations which I have chronicled in *Rural England*, no person is more alive than myself to the vital need to the nation of keeping our best blood within our shores. How can it be otherwise in a country whereof, I am informed, but one-seventh of the population now remains upon the land, the rest being heaped up in the urban districts?

Also the subject should be considered from the point of view of the safety of the Nation. It is not pleasant for Englishmen to read such reports on the quality of our soldiers as one that appeared in the columns of the *Times* not a month ago :—

" They were not men, and were not of the type and condition that ever will grow into men. . . . It is doubtful if more than 50 per cent. of the Line Infantry present on Laffan's Plain could have endured the parade if they had been in full marching order. Yet of what value would an infantryman be in war against Continental troops if he could not stand half a day with 60 lb. on his back? . . . When one sees the fine type of robust and intelligent young fellow that the Yeomanry draws, and compares him with the puny pigmy whom we have to pamper to procure at all, one realises that our system of recruiting is wrong."

Yes, and for an obvious reason. If the writer in the *Times* were to pursue his investigations he would, I think, discover that the great majority of these " puny pigmies " spring from towns or town-bred parents, while the " robust and intelligent " yeomen are country born.

With these few comments I must perforce leave this branch of the matter.

There are, however, other faces to it of which I am free to speak. Thus : to object to the emigration of suitable persons from the cities of the United Kingdom to various parts of the Empire where they are needed seems to me unreasonable and unsound. For that they are not needed in those cities is, as every rate-payer knows, unfortunately but too evident. What may be the exact sum of individuals who are partially or wholly supported by parish relief and charity in Great Britain and Ireland in any given year I am not sure, but it must be well over a million.[1]

Every winter we see the same sights and hear the same voices, which, summed up, paint one picture and echo one chorus—heart-rending poverty, inconceivable misery, national degeneration, perplexity and despair. Even in the midst of summer the unemployed of Leicester march upon London, and thence, poor creatures, are marched back again no richer and no happier than they started. Moreover, just above and merging with the class who are forced to expose their bitter need to the relieving-officer, are other hordes who drag out existence in a state of piteous destitution, and at length but too often are sucked into the black whirlpool upon whose lips they have struggled so long, that vortex of beggary and destruction whereof the uttermost pit is a pauper's grave.

For instance, in an interval of correcting these proofs, I have just taken up a paper, the *Daily Express*, to look at the news. Here is the first item of it that my eye fell upon under the heading, "How the Poor Live and Die".

It is the story of the inquest on a certain Mrs. Higgs who lived in North London and died shortly after finding pinned upon her door a landlord's notice to quit her room on account of non-payment of rent.

The family consisted of four, Mrs. Higgs, a recent widow, and her three daughters. Their only support

---

[1] The number of persons in receipt of poor law relief (exclusive of that of private charity) on 1st January, 1905 (in England and Wales only) appears to amount to the gigantic total of 932,267, of whom 148,013 lived in London. That is to say, that one in every thirty-six of the population was, at that very recent date, being more or less supported by the public purse. These fearful figures, which of course take no account of the millions of very poor who are not actually in receipt of relief from the rates, tell their own tale and need no comment.—H. R. H.

was half a crown a week earned by the eldest daughter, Emily, aged fourteen, the rent being 3s. 6d. a week, Mrs. Higgs herself having become too ill to work. The verdict of the jury was "Death from Heart Disease, accelerated by want of food".

The sustenance of the family during the week preceding the death consisted, according to the Coroner's officer, of "nothing but bread and dripping, and very often not that". A few weeks previously the fourteen-year-old Emily fell out of work, whereon at last the mother applied for relief, but was only allowed some milk. On Emily reaching her present mature age of fourteen, however, this relief was stopped. Not long afterwards Mrs. Higgs died.

Under all the circumstances it does not seem strange that this poor child should have "burst into tears" in the course of her public examination.

Here is a second instance of a different sort. A servant of my own, an old woman, has a son-in-law, a teetotaller of good character, who has presented the State with nine children, all living. Last February twelvemonth he was discharged from the London gasworks in which he had been employed for fifteen years, on account of the slackness of work. He sought it elsewhere but was refused because of his age, which is fifty years. Indeed I am informed that "he has worn the boots right off his feet in walking about looking for work," but all that he has obtained has been a temporary job which I secured for him through the kind offices of the Salvation Army. Meanwhile he and his wife and children subsist on ten shillings a week allowed to them out of the wages of my servant.

Now, I ask, would not the Higgs family and this man with his nine children be better off upon the vast unoccupied lands of Canada, and would their departure from its shores be any real loss to this country?

Putting aside for the moment the question and possibility of settlement on our Home lands, can it be right to keep so many people with their delicate, outworn women and little children in a state that the imagination of most of us has not the power to appreciate or even to understand? This, too, when if they may but be brought there, there exist millions of acres of fertile soil on which in a few years' time their former condition would become to them but as the memory of some hateful vision of the night? Who will be bold enough to declare that it is right, remembering that if they go, not only do they relieve pressure and benefit themselves, they also benefit our Empire abroad, where, if they be decent folk, their advent will be held a blessing?

Of this latter fact I will take one example, and that an old one. In the year 1820 after a period of great distress in England 6,000 settlers were chosen out of 90,000 applicants to be sent by our Government of that day to the Cape Colony. Everything connected with their emigration was mismanaged in a fashion that I trust would now be impossible, with the result that on arrival after a three months' voyage the settlers underwent great miseries. In some way, however, they found themselves homes, and now their blood is everywhere in South Africa. The issue, put briefly, is that, had those settlers not been sent, I do not believe that the Cape to-day would continue to belong to the British Crown.

May not what has happened in the past occur again? If six, or sixteen, or sixty thousand persons from our towns are emigrated to, let us say, Rhodesia, may not the time come when Britain will owe her continued possession of that country to their presence or to that of their descendants?

This is a digression illustrative of the Imperial side of the affair only, which I know is not popular with every one. Still, regarding it strictly from our home standpoint and leaving the Empire to look after itself, I say that we have no right to keep these people meshed in their net of sorrows, if we are not prepared to afford them the opportunity of leading a life of reasonable decency and comfort in return for the labour of their hands. This, it seems—unless home land-settlement on a large scale is proved to be feasible, and then it could provide for most of them — our circumstances do not make it possible for us to do. Therefore I think it is ethically wrong and even cruel to keep such folk decaying in masses in our towns, seeing their children grow up to lives of uselessness, shame and often sin, if the opportunity does exist of moving numbers of them to happy homes under the British flag elsewhere. Such an opportunity, I maintain, my plan furnishes with very little risk of loss to the nation.

Also they are going away already—tens of thousands of them are going every year, for the most part to foreign countries where they will create wealth and compete with us—the land that bred them and paid for their education and upbringing. Thus I believe that in 1903 123,662, and in 1904 over 100,000 emigrated to the United States alone, many of whom, had my scheme been in operation, might have been diverted to British Colonies. Further, we can well part with a considerable proportion of our poverty-stricken, city-dwelling, middle-aged working men with families who make the best land-settlers and colonists, for rich as we may be, we cannot afford to pension them, which is the only alternative, and if we could, we cannot pension their children. Such folk are not needed by the master farmer or the city employer in any country, therefore the soil, where they are needed as husbandmen on their own account, is their only refuge. Moreover, land-settlement schemes, whether at home or abroad, are the very best form of pension, since when the settler dies he leaves his estate and accumulated property to his children.

It must be remembered too that the single man and the single woman are everywhere driving the married man and woman to the wall, for the employer, being in competition with other employers in all countries, is obliged to do the best he can for himself, and finds that best in the hiring of single folk. Also by removing such middle-aged married people from the field of internecine struggle for mere food and raiment to where the earth will yield them both in plenty, we open a door which must leave a wider field for the young people to occupy and enable them to marry and settle down at home. By the time that such young people have reached the same "too-old-at-forty" stage, we can hope that conditions may have improved and that it will no longer be necessary for them to leave the country in their turn, but should it prove necessary, the same remedy will still be applicable, and they too can be settled on the land either in this kingdom or abroad.

The only other remedy, for we are face to face with hard facts that will not budge, seems to be to break up the home, disposing of the parents in this State or charitable institution and of the children in that, and bearing the burden of their support as best we may. This process has been called "domicide," which in the opinion of many is as bad, or worse, than homicide. Surely "domiculture," the perpetuation of the home and the creation of more homes, is better than this merciless, unnatural and uneconomic proceeding, and to it we should turn in our difficulty. Further, by creating hope in the breasts of those who are left behind, such hope as will come with steady work and the possibility of rising in the world, we offer to them the greatest possible inducement to self-reformation and self-improvement. That many can be improved who are commonly looked upon as lapsed and lost, if suitable means are employed, has been demonstrated again and again. But those means must be at hand, and chief among them is the opportunity of earning an honest living.

On the other hand, there are multitudes who are so deeply sunk in the sloughs of drink, disease and degradation that in fact they cannot be improved. I have been told that my plan is futile because "it does not go to the root of the question," that is because it does not provide for the scum and the dregs of our city society. I admit that this is so, for my scheme is on business, not on pauperising lines; indeed I go further and say that no system formulated by the brain of man can provide for these people except through pure charity, or in the workhouse and the jail.

The adult "dead-beats," "born-tireds," "breakages," "alcoholics," tramps, "hoboes," criminals, "sneaks," "half-wits," dissolute women and the like are for the most part beyond redemption, that is in the sense of turning them into useful and hardworking citizens. With their children something can be done—perhaps; with themselves little or nothing. The generation which has suffered them to arise and haunt the courts and alleys of great towns, must bear the burden of their maintenance. No colony would receive them, nor can it be expected to do so. To employ them at the public expense means scamped work, executed at great cost and trouble; to advance them money to enable them to help themselves means money lost.

Representatives of their stamp are to be found in every class of society, from those of good birth who year after year suck up the savings or the necessary pittance of their mothers, wives and sisters, down to the dangerous, sturdy beggars who do violence, whine or threaten on the roadway, and the wide-coated, spirituous knaves who lear and linger at street corners. All such must be the care of the ministers of religion or of the law, not of those who wish to enable good-hearted or repentant if unfortunate persons to help themselves.

To say therefore that a scheme which would assist thousands and tens of thousands to regain a lost foothold or to find a new one, that would benefit the land, the Country and the Empire and prevent countless children from sinking into death, ill-health, vice or idleness, should be thrust aside as of no worth because it cannot be made to include this evasive and immoral class, is in my humble judgment to say a vain thing. In fact, no such scheme is possible, or so I believe.

There is but one more criticism upon which I need to comment, that which is directed against my proposal that the various Municipalities and Boards of Guardians of the Poor-law Unions might be asked to contribute towards the Emigration or Settlement funds, should they choose to do so. The argument is that nothing of the sort should be allowed, because it would increase the rates and discredit the whole movement. I confess that it is one which I cannot follow; indeed I doubt whether my position has been correctly apprehended by these critics. The contributions I have suggested would be of a purely voluntary nature, and whether or not it might prove more expensive to keep families for long periods of time out of the rates, or to pay a lump sum down and be rid of the burden for ever, is a matter of calculation which each Board or other Corporate Authority could work out for itself.

One point I have overlooked, namely, the contention that it would be unjust to confine the benefits of any land-settlement scheme to the inhabitants of cities, since agricultural labourers and other country dwellers have an equal claim to all such advantages. This may be so, but at present it is the city problem which I was directed to consider; also I may remark that to employ such agencies for the purpose of emigrating farm labourers would be to increase that depopulation of the English soil which is so mischievous and so widely deplored. The possibility of setting up industrious rural workers upon small holdings of their own I will not discuss here, as it belongs to a part of the question from which I am debarred. But that it is quite possible under certain conditions, I have small doubt.

It only remains for me to add that I trust that all who are interested in these very important matters will be at the pains to read the following Report and its accompanying documents and to judge of them for themselves. It little becomes an author to speak of his own work, yet under the special circumstances I will be bold enough to say that those who ponder my pages patiently and impartially, even if they do not agree with all of them, may perhaps find therein some spark of leading light.

So I think, at least, who have studied these problems for many years and during the last six months have given to them an attention so complete that, if it is to be continued indefinitely—and great reforms on which the whole heart is set are ill company to be rid of—may, it has occurred to me, in the end prove somewhat perplexing to a person with other obligations to fulfil. At least, believing thoroughly in my conclusions, I submit them with humility and respect to the consideration of my fellow - countrymen. This I do in the hope that perhaps a sufficient consensus of public opinion may be evoked to induce our Government to take some really broad and effective action towards the attainment of the object that I have set before myself, namely, the lessening of our difficulties and of the miseries of our poor by the transference of those who may prove suitable and willing among them from their darksome city dens to the depopulated lands of the

United Kingdom or to the fertile and uninhabited wastes of the Empire overseas.

I admit, however, that I am not too sanguine of success, for in this country, stiff-jointed as it is with age, we cannot stoop readily to a new idea. Nor is it to be expected that the Government of the United Kingdom will prove as generous and as open to conviction as I found that of the Dominion. For example, as regards the Salvation Army and its capacities, I, who have seen, may *know* the truth, but to convey that sure and certain knowledge to minds pre-occupied with many important matters, is no easy task. In Canada also, where week by week they behold this same Salvation Army disembarking its quota of emigrants and conducting them, thousand after thousand, without scandal, hitch or mismanagement, every man to the situation that has been found for him, they may and do appreciate its quality. But here, though multitudes of the poor could tell him better, what does the mention of the Salvation Army suggest to the average educated person? A vision of poke bonnets and military caps worn by professors of " corybantic Christianity " and all kinds of music—no more!

This is one of the reasons why my suggestions as to their employment for these great purposes are sometimes greeted with a tolerant and superior smile. "Make use of a set of cranks ! It is absurd ! Keep clear of all the tribes of religious fanatics, whatever they call themselves "—and so on.

One hears little of such talk in Canada and the United States, where, to the public knowledge, these " cranks," though they number " not many mighty, not many noble," are fulfilling their great and self-imposed office with a whole-hearted humility and patience worthy of the first founders of the Christian faith.

There are so many different voices to be heard

also, so many divergent interests to be reconciled. One party would allow of no rural Settlement unless the whole of our system of land tenure is first passed through the fire of Revolution, a proviso which must postpone everything till the Greek Kalends. Another, that of the Socialists, seems to object to Emigration on principle and clamours for State employment at high wages for all who seek relief. The Exchequer authorities look askance on general grounds at the guaranteeing of loans for any purpose, even if those loans can be repaid. Royal Commissions and Departmental Committees have before now proved themselves to be splendid sextons, and even if their reports are favourable, they do not often lead to efficient legislative action. Religious, yes, and Social Organisations, cry out against other Organisations and will see no good in them or their methods. And so forth.

In the storm of all these forces blowing from east and west and north and south, it may well happen therefore that my ark of refuge will founder as others have before: that nothing effectual will be done. And if nothing is done, what then? Every winter a clamour and a crisis with wild threats and violence, appeased for the hour by ever-increasing inroads on the rates and other public funds. Then when the next winter comes the same desperate, ominous shapes of Misery and Want, and in their hands the swords of Socialism.

Still I possess my soul in patience and with pen and tongue humbly labour on by every avenue that is open to me, greatly comforted from time to time by the "hearty sympathy" of such prescient leaders of men as Mr. Roosevelt, President of the United States, who writes to me after studying my Report that he agrees "absolutely" with my purpose and the general outline of my plan. Still I hope that some day the Nation will come to understand that the true cure or palliative for these and many other troubles is to be found, not in workhouses or in other State-supported institutions, but upon the land, whether it be the land of Britain or that of her immeasurable Empire, which between them, were our poor ten times as many, could provide for every one, and, understanding, will insist, before it is too late, upon some well-weighed and general application of this simple remedy.

May we venture to hope that the new Royal Commission which is to be appointed to consider the working of the Poor-Law and kindred matters will consent to consider this solution of the problem ?

H. RIDER HAGGARD.

Ditchingham, 1st July, 1905.

CONTENTS.

INTRODUCTION . . . . **v**

Serial No.	From and to whom.	Date.	Subject.	Page.
i.	To Mr. H. Rider Haggard.	31st January, 1905.	Nominates him as Commissioner to inspect and report on the Salvation Army agricultural and industrial establishments in the United States of America and conveys instructions.	**xxxix**
ii.	Mr. H. Rider Haggard.	1st February, 1905.	Accepts with thanks the nomination in No. i. ; notes instructions and submits suggestions.	**xl**
iii.	To Mr. H. Rider Haggard.	7th February, 1905.	Concurs that if the Salvation Army experiments commend themselves to him he may make practical suggestions for the projected transfer of urban populations of the United Kingdom to different parts of the British Empire.	**xli**

MR. RIDER HAGGARD'S REPORT.

1	To the Secretary of State for the Colonies from Commissioner H. Rider Haggard.	5th May, 1905.	Report on the Salvation Army Colonies in the United States, and at Hadleigh, England, with scheme of National Land Settlement and general remarks by Commissioner H. Rider Haggard.	1
2	Ditto.	11th March, 1905.	Notes * of conversation between President Roosevelt and H. Rider Haggard.	

* Not Printed.

CONTENTS

Serial No.	From and to whom.	Date.	Subject.	Page.
3	To the Secretary of State for the Colonies from Commissioner H. Rider Haggard.	8th March, 1905.	Notes of interview between the Honourable James Wilson, Secretary of Agriculture for the United States, and H. Rider Haggard.	28
4	From Commissioner H. Rider Haggard to Sir Wilfrid Laurier, Prime Minister of the Government of Canada.	13th April, 1905.	Asking Sir Wilfrid Laurier whether the Government of the Dominion of Canada would be prepared to donate a tract of suitable land for the purpose of the settlement of carefully selected families taken from among the poor of Great Britain, and stating that this communication is made entirely on his own responsibility.	31
5	From Governor-General Earl Grey to Sir Wilfrid Laurier.	13th April, 1905.	Letter to Sir Wilfrid Laurier covering that of even date from H. Rider Haggard.	32
6	From Sir Wilfrid Laurier to H. Rider Haggard.	10th April, 1905. (This is an error — the letter was written on 14th April, 1905.— H. R. H.)	Acknowledging receipt of letter from H. Rider Haggard of 13th April, and stating that he will have much pleasure in discussing the project written of therein.	33
7	From the Honourable Clifford Sifton to H. Rider Haggard.	16th April, 1905.	Approving of Commissioner H. Rider Haggard's scheme of Land Settlement, offering to serve upon a Canadian Committee in order to carry it out, and stating that he regards this scheme as an embodiment of the truest and best form of Imperial patriotism.	34
8	From H. Rider Haggard to the Honourable Clifford Sifton.	17th April, 1905.	Agreeing with the views expressed by the Honourable Clifford Sifton and expressing the hope that, after reflection, the Canadian Government will see its way to assisting in the matter of a guarantee of the capital necessary to put the Immigration Scheme into operation in Canada.	35

CONTENTS xxxiii

Serial No.	From and to whom.	Date.	Subject.	Page.
9	From Sir Wilfrid Laurier to Commissioner H. Rider Haggard.	17th April, 1905.	Despatch to Commissioner H. Rider Haggard, stating that the Government of Canada will be prepared at any time to set aside ten townships (240,000 acres) for the objects set forth by the said H. Rider Haggard. Stating further that if the experiment proves successful other lands will no doubt be available, and that the Government of Canada is satisfied that if a proper class of settlers is secured such a scheme as that propounded by the said H. Rider Haggard ought to be completely successful. Expressing the hope of the Government of Canada also that the said H. Rider Haggard will be allowed to carry it to completion.	36
10	From Commissioner H. Rider Haggard to Sir Wilfrid Laurier.	17th April, 1905.	Acknowledging despatch from Sir Wilfrid Laurier of equal date, thanking the Government of Canada for their liberal offer, and stating that the same will at once be laid by him before the Imperial Government.	37
11	To Secretary of State for the Colonies, from Commissioner H. Rider Haggard.	—	Remarks by Commissioner H. Rider Haggard on the Fort Romie Colony of the Salvation Army in California, United States of America.	38
12	Ditto.	27th March, 1905.	Verbatim notes of interview between Commissioner H. Rider Haggard and various officers of the Salvation Army held at the Fort Romie Colony.	45
13	Ditto.	27th and 28th March, 1905.	Notes of interviews between Commissioner H. Rider Haggard and the Colonists on the Fort Romie Colony.	55
14	Ditto.	29th March, 1905.	Affidavit of Thomas Holland re prices paid for land at Fort Romie, etc., sworn to before Adeline Copeland, Notary Public.	62

CONTENTS

Serial No.	From and to whom.	Date.	Subject.	Page.
15	To Secretary of State for the Colonies, from Commissioner H. Rider Haggard.	29th March, 1905.	Affidavit from W. H. H. Metz, Supervisor of Monterey County, California, as to valuation of Fort Romie Colony.	62
16	To the Secretary of State for the Colonies from Commissioner H. Rider Haggard.	29th March, 1905.	Affidavit of W. H. Bingaman, Real Estate and Insurance Broker, of Soledad, California, as to the valuation of Fort Romie Colony.	63
17	Ditto.	29th March, 1905.	Valuation by W. H. H. Metz and W. H. Bingaman of Land, Plant, Buildings, Water Supply, Stock and Crop on Fort Romie Colony.	63
18	Ditto.	1st April, 1905.	Statement showing the financial position of the colonists of the Salvation Army, Fort Romie Colony.	66
19	Ditto.	—	Remarks by Commissioner H. Rider Haggard on the Fort Amity Colony of the Salvation Army in Colorado, United States of America.	67
20	Ditto.	5th April, 1905.	Verbatim notes of interview between Commissioner H. Rider Haggard and various officers of the Salvation Army held at the Fort Amity Colony.	73
21	Ditto.	5th, 6th and 7th April, 1905.	Notes of interviews between Commissioner H. Rider Haggard and the Colonists on the Fort Amity Colony.	83
22	Ditto.	7th April, 1905.	Affidavit by F. de la Tour Booth Tucker and Alfred Hamon as to the correctness of figures furnished re valuation, etc., of Fort Amity Colony.	102
23	Ditto.	7th April, 1905.	Affidavit by Joseph S. McMurtry as to the correctness of his valuation of the Fort Amity Salvation Army Colony.	102

CONTENTS

Serial No.	From and to whom.	Date.	Subject.	Page.
24	To the Secretary of State for the Colonies from Commissioner H. Rider Haggard.	1st April, 1905.	Statement showing financial position of Fort Amity Colony (not including Colonists' holdings) as per valuation made by J. S. McMurtry and duly sworn.	104
25	Ditto.	1st April, 1905.	Further statement showing financial condition of the Fort Amity Colony as per valuation made by J. S. McMurtry and duly sworn.	106
26	Ditto.	—	Short histories of the Amity Colonists.	108
27	Ditto.	4th April, 1905.	Statement showing the financial position of the Colonists of the Salvation Army Fort Amity Colony.	110
28	Ditto.	—	Memorandum of information respecting the Salvation Army Colony at Fort Amity.	111
29	Ditto.	10th April, 1905.	Remarks by Commissioner H. Rider Haggard on the Fort Herrick Colony of the Salvation Army in Ohio, U.S.A.	115
30	Ditto.	9th April, 1905.	Verbatim notes of interview between Commissioner H. Rider Haggard, Commander Booth Tucker, and Colonel Higgins, of the Salvation Army, as to the Fort Herrick Colony of the Salvation Army in Ohio, U.S.A.	119
31	To Commander Booth Tucker of the Salvation Army from Commissioner H. Rider Haggard.	20th April, 1905.	Asking officially for various assurances from the Salvation Army.	122
32	From Commander Booth Tucker of the Salvation Army to Commissioner H. Rider Haggard.	24th April, 1905.	Giving the assurances asked for by Commissioner H. Rider Haggard in his communication of 20th April, 1905.	123

CONTENTS

Serial No.	From and to whom.	Date.	Subject.	Page.
33	To the Secretary of State for the Colonies from Commissioner H. Rider Haggard.	24th April, 1905.	Remarks by Commissioner H. Rider Haggard on the Salvation Army Colony at Hadleigh, in Essex, England.	126
34	To the Secretary of State for the Colonies from Commissioner H. Rider Haggard.	—	Remarks by Commissioner H. Rider Haggard on the work of the Vacant Lots Cultivation Association at Philadelphia, U.S.A.	137
35	Ditto.	—	Estimated cost in Pounds Sterling of Canadian Colonisation Scheme exclusive of value of land.	141
36	Ditto.	—	Approximate statement showing annual charges, income and probable surplus of Canadian Colonisation Scheme.	142
37	Ditto.	—	Approximate statement showing security for loan to carry out suggested Canadian Colonisation Scheme.	143
38	To Commissioner H. Rider Haggard from Earl Grey, Governor-General of Canada. (Telegraphic.)	19th April, 1905.	Expressing the hope that Commissioner H. Rider Haggard's report may weave Canada closer than ever to England, and be the means of providing happy homes for thousands who, without hope, throng the city life of Great Britain.	144

PRESS OPINIONS 145

LIST OF ILLUSTRATIONS.

Irrigation Ditch, Fort Romie . . . . *Frontispiece*

Irrigation Flume, Fort Romie . . . . ,,

Children at Play, Fort Romie . . . . *To face page* 38

General View of Fort Romie . . . . ,, 38

The Sanatorium, Fort Amity . . . , . . . ,, 67

Colonist's Cottage, Fort Amity . . . . ,, 67

A Group of Colonists, Fort Amity . . . . . . ,, 88

Colonists Harvesting Kafir Corn . . . . . . ,, 83

Infants' School, Fort Amity . . . . ,, 104

Town Site Stores, Fort Amity . . . . ,, 104

Colonist's House, Fort Romie . . . . ,, 141

Colonist's House, Fort Romie . . . . ,, 141

COLONIAL OFFICE TO MR. H. RIDER HAGGARD.

Downing Street, 31st January, 1905.

SIR,

I AM directed by Mr. Secretary Lyttelton to inform you that he has nominated you to be a Commissioner to proceed to the United States and to inspect and report to him upon the conditions and character of the agricultural and industrial settlements which have been established there by the Salvation Army, with a view to the transmigration of suitable persons from the great cities of the United States to the land and the formation of agricultural communities.

2. It appears to the Secretary of State that, if these experiments are found to be successful, some analogous system might, with great advantage, be applied in transferring the urban populations of the United Kingdom to different parts of the British Empire.

3. You should pay special attention to the class of persons taken by the Salvation Army, their training and success as agricultural settlers, and the general effect upon character and social happiness : you should also consider the financial aspect of the experiments.

4. It would be desirable that after you have inspected the several settlements you should proceed to Ottawa and discuss the subject with Lord Grey, who has taken great interest in it, as well as with such local authorities as may be indicated to you by the Governor-General as likely to aid you with advice and assistance as to the application of the system in a British Colony.

5. The Rhodes Trustees, with whom the suggestion of the inquiry originated, and by whom Mr. Lyttelton has been asked to nominate a Commissioner, have made a grant of £300, including all travelling expenses, to meet the cost of the inquiry.

I am, etc.,
FRED. GRAHAM.

No. ii.

MR. H. RIDER HAGGARD TO COLONIAL OFFICE.

(Received 2nd February, 1905.)

Ditchingham House, Norfolk, 1st February, 1905.

SIR,

I HAVE the honour to acknowledge the receipt of your letter of 31st January wherein you inform me that I have been nominated by Mr. Secretary Lyttelton to be a Commissioner to proceed to the United States for certain purposes which you detail and to report to him thereon.

2. I take this opportunity to offer to the Secretary of State my thanks for the confidence he has placed in me and to express the hope that I shall be able to carry out my mission to his satisfaction.

3. With reference to paragraph 2 of your communication, I presume that, in the event of my investigation showing me that these experiments in land settlement are in fact successful and that their principle is capable of wide application, it is wished that I should include in my report any practical suggestions that occur to me as to the means and methods whereby the example might best be turned to use in order to relieve the pressure upon our urban populations, and at the same time advantage other portions of the Empire.

4. I note the various instructions which you convey to me and will obey the same.

5. I have booked passages for myself and my daughter, Miss Angela Rider Haggard, who accompanies me as my secretary, upon the *Teutonic*, which sails on the 22nd instant.

I am, etc.,

H. RIDER HAGGARD.

No. III.

COLONIAL OFFICE TO MR. H. RIDER HAGGARD.

Downing Street, 7th February, 1905.

SIR,

I AM directed by Mr. Secretary Lyttelton to acknowledge the receipt of your letter of the 1st instant notifying your acceptance of the commission to proceed to the United States of America to report on the Salvation Army agricultural and industrial settlements established in that country and to express his concurrence in your suggestion that in the event of the experiments by the Salvation Army commending themselves to you, you should include in your report any practical suggestions which may occur to you as to the means and methods whereby the example might best be turned to use in connection with the projected transfer of urban populations of the United Kingdom to different parts of the British Empire.

2. I am to inform you that the Government of the United States will be requested, through the proper channel, to afford such facilities as may be possible for the furtherance of your mission.

I am, etc.,

FRED. GRAHAM.

REPORT

AND

SCHEME OF NATIONAL LAND SETTLEMENT

BY

COMMISSIONER H. RIDER HAGGARD.

No. 1.

Sir,

1. I HAVE the honour to report that, in pursuance of instructions received from you under dates 31st January, 1905, and 7th February, 1905, I proceeded to the United States of America, and there visited the Salvation Army Land Colonies, situated respectively at Fort Romie, California, Fort Amity, Colorado, and Fort Herrick, Ohio. Of these Colonies full descriptions will be found under their separate headings, and with them minutes of conferences which I held with Officers of the Salvation Army at each place, notes of interviews with the Colonists, various sworn valuations, and other statistics and documents.

2. Also, during my travels in the States, I investigated at Philadelphia the plan of Vacant Lot Cultivation there in force, of which I append a descriptive note, while at Washington the system of irrigation and land settlement which, under a recent Act, has been inaugurated by the Government of the United States, was explained to me by Mr. F. H. Newell, Engineer of the United States Geological Survey and Superintendent of the Reclamation Service. This system I was enabled to study at various places, especially at Yuma,

in Arizona (where I was detained for some days by a "wash-out" of the Colorado River).

3. Further, at Salt Lake City, I collected information from the President and other Authorities of the Mormon Church as to their methods of Land Settlement by "small holders," of whose tidy and prosperous farms I saw many.

4. At Washington I had interviews with President Roose-velt and with Mr. Wilson, Secretary of Agriculture. Of these interviews I attach notes to this report, those describing that with Mr. Secretary Wilson, which have been submitted for his approval and passed by him as accurate, for publica-tion, and those of my interesting conversation with Mr. Roosevelt for your private information only,[1] as in this instance the summary, although I believe it to be quite correct, has not been perused by him, nor have I asked his permission to print the same.

5. Having finished my business in the United States, I proceeded to Ottawa, where, after a long and arduous journey round the Continent, I arrived on the 13th April, 1905, and, with my daughter, was invited by His Excellency Earl Grey, the Governor-General of Canada, to be his guest at Govern-ment House. During my visit to Ottawa I had various interviews with Sir Wilfrid Laurier, G.C.M.G., the Prime Minister of the Canadian Government; the Honourable Clifford Sifton, till recently Minister of the Interior, a states-man of much experience and authority; Mr. R. L. Borden, the leader of the Opposition; the Honourable W. S. Field-ing, Minister of Finance; Mr. W. D. Scott, Superintendent of Immigration; Doctor Bryce, Medical Officer of Immigra-tion; Professor Robertson, the well-known educational au-thority; Mr. White, of the Canadian Pacific Railway, and others.

6. Also, I addressed a distinguished and earnest gathering of about four hundred members of the Canadian Club on subjects connected with Land Settlement, at a luncheon which was given in my honour and in that of Commander Booth Tucker, of the Salvation Army, who journeyed from England to meet me at Fort Amity, and accompanied me to Ottawa.

[1] Not printed.

7. The results of these conferences are very clearly shown in the documents which I append to this report. These are :—

   (a) Letter from Commissioner H. Rider Haggard to the Right Honourable Sir Wilfrid Laurier, dated 13th April.

   (b) Letter from His Excellency Earl Grey to the Right Honourable Sir Wilfrid Laurier, covering my communication of the same date.

   (c) Letter from Sir Wilfrid Laurier to H. Rider Haggard, dated in error 10th April, but in reality written on the 14th in answer to his of the 13th.

   (d) Letter from the Honourable Clifford Sifton to H. Rider Haggard, dated 16th April.

   (e) Answer from H. Rider Haggard to the Honourable Clifford Sifton, dated 17th April.

   (f) Despatch from the Right Honourable Sir Wilfrid Laurier to Commissioner H. Rider Haggard, dated 17th April.

   (g) Despatch from Commissioner H. Rider Haggard to the Right Honourable Sir Wilfrid Laurier of even date.

8. These documents accurately set out the progress and successful conclusion of my discussions with the Canadian Government. I will, however, comment upon them briefly.

By working in the trains I was enabled roughly to draft my reports upon the Land Colonies in time to submit the same to the Governor-General and his Ministers upon my arrival at Ottawa. His Excellency studied these and the documents annexed to them very thoroughly. Considering them satisfactory, he announced that he was prepared to commend to the favourable consideration of his Ministers the views and suggestions which I had the honour to lay before him. These included a request for a free grant of land from the Canadian Government suitable for settlement, and amounting in area to not less than ten townships or 240,000 acres (say, 360 square miles), with a promise of extra land to be given if necessary in the future. This area, allowing 160 acres per family, which is the ordinary Canadian homestead

lot, would accommodate about 1,500 families, or, if an average of five persons is reckoned per family, 7,500 souls.

The cost of the transportation and the settling of that
number of people in Canada, where the land is given, may,
I think, be put down roughly at about £200 per family, or
£300,000 in all. This, however, is only an approximate,
not a final estimate.

In addition to the land grant, if I could obtain the same,
I sought an expression of the willingness of the Canadian
Government, at any rate to a certain extent, to assist in
guaranteeing the interest on a loan which would provide the
capital necessary to put my settlement scheme, if approved,
into operation in the Dominion.

It will be seen from the Prime Minister's despatch of
17th April that, so far as regards the former of these requests,
I have succeeded beyond my expectations, inasmuch as the
Canadian Government, under the authority of His Excellency the Governor-General in Council, states therein that
it is prepared at any time to give ten townships for the
object propounded by me, on the sole consideration that the
liberal conditions of settlement prescribed by the laws of
Canada be complied with. It states further that the Prime
Minister has no doubt that his Government will be disposed
to set aside other tracts of land under similar conditions, the
selection of all such land, and this is a very important boon,
being left entirely to the judgment of the Commissioner
appointed by His Majesty's Government, who would, however, be assisted in his labours by the expert agents of the
Canadian Government.

It adds that the Government of Canada is satisfied that
if a proper class of settlers be secured such a scheme as I
have in mind ought to be completely successful, a conclusion
which I must regard as most satisfactory.

With this scheme I will deal later.

9. As regards the second point, namely, that of obtaining
a limited monetary guarantee from the Canadian Government, I regret to report that in this matter I have, up to
the present, failed to secure any such guarantee.

At a conference which I held with the Honourable W. S.
Fielding, Minister of Finance, at Government House, on the
17th April, however, he told me that he would consult with

his colleagues on the question, and, perhaps, write or cable to me their further views. This was as far as I was able to take the matter, nor do I wish it to be understood that anything definite passed thereon, although that it is to be further considered is doubtless a gain.

10. I venture to suggest, therefore, that, should it wish to proceed with this great scheme, the Imperial Government might with advantage communicate with the Government of Canada and lay before it any opinions they may form upon this point. That the Government of Canada has acted with much liberality in making so splendid an offer of valuable free land there is no doubt, but I dare to hope that if formally approached they may yet prove disposed to add to it by facilitating the raising of a loan in conjunction with the Imperial Treasury, especially as I can see little reason to fear that any permanent financial risk or burden would thereby be incurred by the guarantors, whoever they may be. It may be thought desirable, however, that any such loan should be guaranteed by the Imperial Government only.

11. I would call especial attention to the Honourable Mr. Sifton's letter of the 16th April to myself, as it is a document of no small importance; also to my answer to the same of the 17th April, wherein I put before him briefly the views which I have expressed above on the question of a guarantee of capital. I will premise my remarks upon this letter by saying that on all such subjects no statesman in Canada carries more weight, or, by common consent, has greater experience or a sounder judgment, than the Honourable Mr. Sifton. To his appreciation of my scheme, indeed, I am largely indebted for whatever measure of success may be held to have attended my discussions with the Canadian Government.

It will be observed that after reading my reports and the other documents, and listening to the arguments which I submitted to him and to the officials and experts whom I approached, Mr. Sifton says that he is convinced that this scheme has the promise of success. Further, he offers to be a member of a Canadian Committee to assist in the carrying of it out. He adds these remarkable, and in every way most encouraging words :—

" I regard your scheme as an embodiment of the truest

and best form of Imperial patriotism, because it is building for the future by helping to give a solid British basis to the population of our great West ".

This is a sentiment with which, as I have said in my answer, I heartily agree. Should the plan come to fruition I humbly submit that the Imperial Government would do wisely to avail itself of Mr. Sifton's proffered assistance.

12. Having made these comments upon my discussions with the Canadian Government, in pursuance of the authority which you have given me so to do, I will now proceed in general terms to outline the plan which I have evolved for putting into practice upon a large scale the principles that underlie the Land Settlements of the Salvation Army in the United States. Before doing so, however, I think it may be advantageous if I make a few general comments upon those Settlements, summarising the information and views which will be found set out in full in my Remarks upon Fort Amity and Fort Romie.

13. As may be gathered from my observations upon these Colonies I am very glad to be able on the whole to give a favourable report of them. Fort Herrick, the third place which I was directed to visit, although it has been called a Colony, is, in reality, at any rate at present, little more than a farm where experimental work is being carried on, and a home for inebriates. For the purposes of this report, therefore, it may in practice be omitted.

A study of my Remarks will show that both at Fort Amity and Fort Romie certain mistakes have been made and certain failures incurred. The system of finance practised by the Salvation Army in reference to its Land Settlements is one that I found somewhat difficult to unravel. I believe, however, although there may still be minor discrepancies and mistakes, that finally I fathomed it, and it will be noticed that the sworn figures given to me show upon these two Colonies a total loss of, roughly speaking, about £10,000. In the case of Fort Romie the loss was incurred during the first abortive settlement, which having been rather rashly undertaken before the land was thoroughly irrigated, was brought to an end by a great and prolonged drought.

In the case of Fort Amity it was due to the necessity of unexpected expenditure and to unforeseen difficulties arising from the character and peculiarities of the soil, as will be found more fully explained in the record of my investigation of that Colony. Also a portion of it in either case must be set down to the high rate of interest at which the Salvation Army borrows money, these settlements having been financed almost entirely by means of loaned capital. Lastly, so far as I was able to discover, certain sums have been charged against the Colonies' account which, strictly speaking, it should not have been called upon to bear.

I will add at once that when the remarkable results achieved are taken into consideration, this loss, in my opinion, is insignificant, and, indeed, is more than counterbalanced by the great value of the experience gained. Moreover, it seems to me that had a somewhat heavier charge been made against the Colonists for their land, as, under the circumstances, should have been done in fairness to the Army, notwithstanding the early difficulties encountered, no loss at all would have been incurred.

That the price asked from these Colonists was too low is, I think, proved by the very considerable " equities " which, it will be observed, they have acquired after a few years' settlement ; that is by the surplus value of their assets over all their liabilities to the Salvation Army and others. (See Remarks on Fort Romie and Fort Amity.) When their accounts show so large a gain, surely that of the Salvation Army ought not, in justice, to be debited with a loss.

Outside of this slight failure of finance, which will, I believe, be recognised as temporary, accidental, and easy to be avoided in future enterprises, the two experiments seem to me to be eminently successful, and to demonstrate, in the case of Fort Romie, that indigent people of the agricultural labourer class can be settled upon land and there do well, and in the case of Fort Amity that such persons can even be taken from towns and yet prosper. I think that a careful perusal of the annexed documents will support my opinions on this matter.

14. Unless, therefore, those opinions are unsound or the conclusions I deduce from them can be shown to be erroneous, it seems evident that from these particular examples may be extracted lessons that are easy of application upon any scale which is desired.

15. The first of these lessons is to avoid the mistakes of the past, especially by refusing to attempt any further settlement unless sufficient capital is available to inaugurate and to carry it on upon proved and business-like principles. The second is that the land should be cheap as well as suitable. The third that the Colonists should be very carefully selected, all the circumstances and conditions of the individual families being considered. The fourth that they should pay a fair price for their land, spread, however, over a considerable number of years ; and the fifth, perhaps the most important of them all, that they should remain during that period under skilled, but sympathetic management. Markets also, with the accessibility and convenience of location, should be borne in mind, while the principle of settlement in communities ought, in my judgment, to receive strict adherence as it has many social and other advantages. I may add that possibly it might be found wise to form the individual communities of persons collected from the same town, or district.

Given these requisites, it will, I consider, be strange if success is not attained even in the case of poor persons taken from the cities, provided that they are steady in character, the victims of misfortune and circumstances rather than of vice ; having had some acquaintance or connection with the land in their past lives, and having also an earnest desire to raise themselves and their children in the world.

Any scheme, therefore, that is to succeed should, in my judgment, provide for the fulfilment of these essentials, at any rate to a large extent.

16. I will now outline the plan which I have evolved, although first I wish to make it clear that if it is held to be inadequate or faulty no one is responsible for it except myself, its author. On the other hand, I may mention that various very able and experienced gentlemen to whom I sketched my suggestions, such as President Roosevelt, Mr. Wilson, Sir Wilfrid Laurier, and Mr. Sifton, appear to have thought them workable and sound.

These suggestions are as follows :—

17. That a sufficient loan, whereof the exact amount may be decided hereafter, or rather the interest on such loan, shall be guaranteed by His Majesty's Government, or, in

cases where the Governments of individual Colonies are willing to co-operate, by His Majesty's Government and such Colonies jointly; it being agreed that each Colony shall share in the benefits of the Land Settlements to be made under the loan in proportion to the amount of its guarantee plus the value of its land grants.

The absolute necessity of such a loan by whomsoever guaranteed is obvious, but if further arguments in its favour are needed they will be found in the histories of Fort Romie and Fort Amity which the Salvation Army have acquired and developed on credit, by means of money borrowed at 5 per cent. and 6 per cent., thereby incurring the greater part of their loss. If land settlement is to be successful it must be conducted upon the strictest business lines, such as would be adopted if the building of a railway or any other industrial enterprise were concerned, and these, of course, include the provision of sufficient capital at a reasonable rate of interest.

If such capital is not forthcoming it would be better to leave the scheme untouched, since to undertake it relying upon what I may call a Trust-in-Providence system of finance will be to court disaster, and possibly to throw the movement back for many years. Nor can the gifts and contributions of the rich, or any other form of charity, which is often fickle in its preferences and uncertain in its action, be depended on in such a case. To relieve our congested cities, and place those that are suitable among their people upon the empty or depopulated lands of the British Empire is a work which the Empire should undertake for its own general good. Nor, in my opinion, need it fear that it will lose by this venture, even in money, for which the land settled and the improvements thereon would be the security, while its gain in other directions must be very great.

18. When this question of a guarantee comes up for discussion, however, it will be well worthy of consideration as to whether the large Municipalities of the United Kingdom should not be asked in what shape they would be prepared to assist the movement so far as the law allows, or by emendation can be made to allow. Probably they could best do this by promising a fixed sum towards the expenses of any indigent but deserving and suitable family who might

be taken off their rates. The same suggestion applies to the Poor Law Unions throughout the land. Of course all such contributions would be purely voluntary, but that difficulty might to some extent be met by giving preference in the matter of the emigration of families to those towns and Unions which elect to pay such contributions.

19. The capital being provided, I suggest that a permanent Imperial Officer should be appointed, to be known as the Superintendent of Land Settlements, or by some similar title. In him these capital sums should be vested as a Corporation Sole, as a trustee for the Government. Or, if it were thought more secure and desirable, the money might stand to the credit of a Board, whereof this Superintendent of Land Settlements was a member, which Board might possibly be formed of himself, the Agents-General of the Colonies, and representatives from the Colonial Office and the Treasury.

The actual administration of the funds, however, should, in my opinion, and subject to proper audit, be left to the judgment of the Superintendent of Land Settlements, upon whose ability, knowledge and method of conducting his business much will depend, especially during the first years of the working of the enterprise.

Here I may say that one of the duties of this official ought to be, in person or by deputy, occasionally to visit and to report upon all Colonies that may be established. The expenses of his salary and office should be a charge upon the Land Settlements Loan, to the satisfactory and economical administration of which it would be his duty to devote himself.

A further and very important part of that duty also would be to stand between the Government and the Charitable Bodies whose part in the business I will explain presently; to receive from them and to check their returns; to investigate any complaints which might be made against them, and if found correct, to remedy the same; to watch that they put no undue religious or sectarian pressure upon the Colonists in the various settlements, let us say in such a matter as the forcing of them to educate the children in a fashion of which their parents did not approve; to be careful that such Charitable Bodies selected the settlers fairly and judiciously from among British subjects only, and so forth.

20. The capital being found, and its safe-guarding and wise management provided for, it will next be convenient to consider the exact objects upon which it should be expended, and how these objects can best be attained.

21. First, what are those objects? To relieve, at any rate to some extent, the congestion of our cities which results in so much degradation, misery and expense to the public, by exporting from them those who are physically, mentally, and in other ways suitable, and who are found to have fallen into, or to be threatened with poverty, or who, being weary of towns, desire to attempt the adventure of a different life in new homes upon the land.

To advantage the Empire by the introduction on to its unoccupied spaces of large numbers of persons whose existence otherwise would have been wasted or worse. Who also, whatever the troubles into which circumstances may have brought them, are of British blood, and the parents of children that will hand down to the future the traditions, characteristics and virtues of our race, which children in new countries will find many opportunities of rising to positions different indeed from their parents' humble state.

22. An obvious criticism of these axioms will be that such persons taken from cities, however willing they may prove to go when in extremity, are not suitable for the purposes of land settlement at home or abroad. Also, that even if they were, it would be difficult, if not impossible, to select them properly, and quite impossible when selected to manage them through that period of years during which they must be nursed into success.

23. The answer is that even in a single great city such as London, where, I believe, last Christmas over 127,000 persons were in receipt of Poor Law Relief, if only hands can be laid upon them, there are numbers of indigent people who are in every way fitted to such purposes. For instance, here may be found many men and women, brought up upon the land, who have drifted to the town, perhaps recently, and failed there, and now in middle life, with a family of young children, would accept with the utmost gratitude the chance of returning to conditions such as formed the company and

surroundings of their youth, and of rectifying their own
mistake by placing their children's feet upon the paths of
prosperity and peace. The same remark applies with even
greater force to provincial towns which are in closer touch
with the rural districts.

"Land," said Commander Booth Tucker, in the interview
which I held with him and others on the 5th April at Fort
Amity, "is abundant throughout the world. The people of
the cities are hungering for the opportunity of getting at it.
They only want leadership and business management. The
only requisite that I see that is absolutely not to be gotten
over is a supply of the necessary capital. Our experience
goes to show that the man without money makes a better
average colonist and a better average settler than the man
with money, and it seems to me a radical mistake that this
and other countries should confine their settlements to the
man with money, and ignore the man whose capital consists
of brain and muscle, but who can be turned into a prosperous
'home-owner'."

With these remarks of Commander Booth Tucker I
entirely agree.

24. It may be admitted, however, that the finding of these
city folk; the selection from among them, and the watching
of those selected for a while before final choice of them is
made, are difficult tasks.   Indeed, if all this had to be
done through officials of any sort, it would in my opinion,
and, I may add, in that of President Roosevelt, be an impossible task, or at the least so costly as to be out of
the question. As it happens, however, a Body exists to
which this matter is easy, that, moreover, is willing to
undertake it for nothing, merely as part of what it considers
to be the duty which it has towards suffering and bewildered
humanity.

I allude to the Salvation Army, a charitable and philanthropic Institution, which I have found even better known
and more respected in the United States and in the Dominion
of Canada than it is in the British Isles. This vast Organisation is, I am authorised to say upon its behalf, able and
willing to make the selection of suitable settlers to any
extent from among the poor of the cities of Great Britain,
conducting their operations under the authority and direction

of an Imperial Officer, appointed, as I have suggested, to
control them.

Further, if only the necessary capital be found, it is prepared to move these selected persons to settlements to be
established at places chosen anywhere within the borders of
the British Empire. There it will provide them with skilled
instruction in the local agriculture, and with the counsel
and assistance needful to beginners in every path of enterprise, which will be furnished to them by means of trained
officers stationed in each Colony, and receiving only the
small remuneration that the Salvation Army pays to its
active members for their support.

25. Upon this point I would call especial attention to
the remarks of Commander Booth Tucker in answer to my
questions which I put to him at Fort Amity. (See Notes
of an interview between Commissioner H. Rider Haggard
and various officers of the Salvation Army at Fort Amity,
Colorado, 5th April, 1905.) I also refer you particularly to
a letter from myself dated 20th April, 1905, to Commander
Booth Tucker as representing the Salvation Army, which is
published with this report, and to his answer, dated 24th
April.

26. To sum up this branch of the matter I believe that
persons with families suitable for settlement (for to such I
suggest preference should be given) can be found in the
cities of the United Kingdom in even greater numbers than
could be dealt with under a really extensive scheme.

27. Thus the capital would be provided, its supervision
would be arranged for, and the Salvation Army, or any other
approved and responsible religious, charitable, or social Organisation, would undertake the selection of the Colonists;
their transportation to their future homes; the building of
their houses and barns; the advance of cash to them for the
purchase of stock, seed, agricultural implements and other
necessaries; their instruction by trained persons in the arts
of husbandry; the collection from them of the amounts due
annually to satisfy the sums advanced and interest thereon;
and their permanent care until everything was paid off and
they could be left masters of their business to pursue their
own destinies free of debt.

In the case of Canada the land also is now provided, and

this without any cost; an example that other British Colonies may be willing to follow in varying degrees.

28. There remain for consideration, however, the matter of safe-guarding the repayment of the capital advanced; also that of the cost of starting such land Settlements. The former of these points will, I consider, prove the crux of this proposed national experiment, since, unless it can be shown that it is possible to carry this out without loss to the guaranteeing Government or Governments, it must break down. Whereas if this can be shown there is absolutely no limit to the possibilities of the scheme.

29. Land settlement cannot be permanently conducted upon the system of a hospital. Its objects should be to teach people to support themselves, and to become useful and productive citizens; not to live upon charity. Moreover, unless it is demonstrated that it can be made to pay its way upon a business basis, no Government or other Authority would continue to guarantee the interest of loans, whereas, if this is demonstrated, after the first step is taken, money will be forthcoming to any extent. Why not? Of capital there is plenty awaiting safe investment at a fair interest, of possible settlers there are plenty, and of land there is plenty also within the broad boundaries of the British Empire, in places where suitable population is often the greatest need.

30. Now, as regards the first of these points, namely, the repayment of the capital, the only actual precedents with which I am acquainted (for I do not propose to deduce arguments from the figures that I append to this report) are to be found in the remarkable New Zealand experiment, which, however, is not the same as that I am advocating, and in the examples of Fort Romie and Fort Amity. Although, as I have shown, small losses were incurred on these Colonies, owing to undercharges as against the settlers, high interest and other mistakes, those examples, I submit, give every ground for hoping that under the conditions which I have set out, the venture of land settlement can be carried through on a sound commercial basis.

31. Still, it should be remembered that each country in which settlements are made will present its own difficulties, that must be overcome by skill, patience and experience.

For all these difficulties in various lands it is impossible to make provision in a preliminary report, since every case must be treated separately, and each danger guarded against by whatever means seem wisest when it arises.

32. Roughly, however, I would propose to follow the example set by that brilliantly successful measure, the New Zealand Advances to Settlers Act. Under this Act I may state that up to the 31st March, 1904, the advances made since about 1895, when it began to operate, amounted to £4,009,520. The securities for the net authorised advances, per contra, were valued at £8,704,640, while the 1 per cent. sinking fund in the hands of a public trustee totalled £158,520. Further, so far as I have been able to discover from the reading of the various documents, no loss whatever was incurred. On the contrary, a considerable profit has been realised.

In the case of this Act a table has been drawn up showing the payments due for every one hundred pounds of the loan advanced, under which the capital lent, and the interest at 5 per cent. are repaid in seventy-three half-yearly instalments; that is, in thirty-six and a half years. This table is so useful and instructive that I include it here.

I have no doubt that with variations, such as local conditions may make necessary in different countries, the above system of proportionate payments can very well be adapted to any scheme of land settlement conducted by means of Government advances.

33. With reference to the cost of starting Colonies, there must be included therein an allowance for the expense, which would often be considerable, of conveying the settlers from the British cities to their new homes in distant lands. Of this cost it is not feasible for me to give an accurate estimate, seeing that it would vary with the mileage over which the emigrants had to be carried, and in accordance with the arrangements that those in charge of them were able to make with steamship and railway companies.

34. I append, however, three tables, numbered 35, 36, 37, and prepared to show, more or less, how a Canadian Scheme of Colonisation might be expected to work out financially upon the basis of a cost of £200 per family of five souls, when, as in the case under consideration, the land would be given free for the purposes of settlement.

TABLE OF PRESCRIBED HALF-YEARLY INSTALMENTS FOR EVERY ONE HUNDRED POUNDS OF THE LOAN.

Half-year.	Prescribed Half-year Instalment.	Apportioned thus :—		Balance of Principal Owing.
		On Account of Interest at Five Per Cent.	On Account of Principal.	
	£ s. d.	£ s. d.	£ s. d.	£ s. d.
1st . . .	3 0 0	2 10 0	0 10 0	99 10 0
2nd . . .	3 0 0	2 9 9	0 10 3	98 19 9
3rd . . .	3 0 0	2 9 6	0 10 6	98 9 3
4th . . .	3 0 0	2 9 3	0 10 9	97 18 6
5th . . .	3 0 0	2 9 0	0 11 0	97 7 6
6th . . .	3 0 0	2 8 8	0 11 4	96 16 2
7th . . .	3 0 0	2 8 5	0 11 7	96 4 7
8th . . .	3 0 0	2 8 1	0 11 11	95 12 8
9th . . .	3 0 0	2 7 10	0 12 2	95 0 6
10th . . .	3 0 0	2 7 6	0 12 6	94 8 0
11th . . .	3 0 0	2 7 2	0 12 10	93 15 2
12th . . .	3 0 0	2 6 11	0 13 1	93 2 1
13th . . .	3 0 0	2 6 7	0 13 5	92 8 8
14th . . .	3 0 0	2 6 3	0 13 9	91 14 11
15th . . .	3 0 0	2 5 10	0 14 2	91 0 9
16th . . .	3 0 0	2 5 6	0 14 6	90 6 3
17th . . .	3 0 0	2 5 2	0 14 10	89 11 5
18th . . .	3 0 0	2 4 9	0 15 3	88 16 2
19th . . .	3 0 0	2 4 5	0 15 7	88 0 7
20th . . .	3 0 0	2 4 0	0 16 0	87 4 7
21st . . .	3 0 0	2 3 7	0 16 5	86 8 2
22nd . . .	3 0 0	2 3 2	0 16 10	85 11 4
23rd . . .	3 0 0	2 2 9	0 17 3	84 14 1
24th . . .	3 0 0	2 2 4	0 17 8	83 16 5
25th . . .	3 0 0	2 1 11	0 18 1	82 18 4
26th . . .	3 0 0	2 1 6	0 18 6	81 19 10
27th . . .	3 0 0	2 1 0	0 19 0	81 0 10
28th . . .	3 0 0	2 0 6	0 19 6	80 1 4
29th . . .	3 0 0	2 0 0	1 0 0	79 1 4
30th . . .	3 0 0	1 19 6	1 0 6	78 0 10
31st . . .	3 0 0	1 19 0	1 1 0	76 19 10
32nd . . .	3 0 0	1 18 6	1 1 6	75 18 4
33rd . . .	3 0 0	1 18 0	1 2 0	74 16 4
34th . . .	3 0 0	1 17 5	1 2 7	73 13 9
35th . . .	3 0 0	1 16 10	1 3 2	72 10 7
36th . . .	3 0 0	1 16 3	1 3 9	71 6 10
37th . . .	3 0 0	1 15 8	1 4 4	70 2 6

TABLE OF PRESCRIBED HALF-YEARLY INSTALMENTS, ETC.—*continued.*

Half-year.	Prescribed Half-year Instalment.	Apportioned thus :—		Balance of Principal Owing.
		On Account of Interest at Five Per Cent.	On Account of Principal.	
	£ s. d.	£ s. d.	£ s. d.	£ s. d.
38th . . .	3 0 0	1 15 1	1 4 11	68 17 7
39th . . .	3 0 0	1 14 5	1 5 7	67 12 0
40th . . .	3 0 0	1 13 10	1 6 2	66 5 10
41st . . .	3 0 0	1 13 2	1 6 10	64 19 0
42nd . . .	3 0 0	1 12 6	1 7 6	63 11 6
43rd . . .	3 0 0	1 11 9	1 8 3	62 3 3
44th . . .	3 0 0	1 11 1	1 8 11	60 14 4
45th . . .	3 0 0	1 10 4	1 9 8	59 4 10
46th . . .	3 0 0	1 9 7	1 10 5	57 14 5
47th . . .	3 0 0	1 8 10	1 11 2	56 3 3
48th . . .	3 0 0	1 8 1	1 11 11	54 11 4
49th . . .	3 0 0	1 7 3	1 12 9	52 18 7
50th . . .	3 0 0	1 6 6	1 13 6	51 5 1
51st . . .	3 0 0	1 5 8	1 14 4	49 10 9
52nd . . .	3 0 0	1 4 9	1 15 3	47 15 6
53rd . . .	3 0 0	1 3 11	1 16 1	45 19 6
54th . . .	3 0 0	1 3 0	1 17 0	44 2 5
55th . . .	3 0 0	1 2 1	1 17 11	42 4 6
56th . . .	3 0 0	1 1 1	1 18 11	40 5 7
57th . . .	3 0 0	1 0 2	1 19 10	38 5 9
58th . . .	3 0 0	0 19 2	2 0 10	36 4 11
59th . . .	3 0 0	0 18 1	2 1 11	34 3 0
60th . . .	3 0 0	0 17 1	2 2 11	32 0 1
61st . . .	3 0 0	0 16 0	2 4 0	29 16 1
62nd . . .	3 0 0	0 14 11	2 5 1	27 11 0
63rd . . .	3 0 0	0 13 9	2 6 3	25 4 9
64th . . .	3 0 0	0 12 7	2 7 5	22 17 4
65th . . .	3 0 0	0 11 5	2 8 7	20 8 9
66th . . .	3 0 0	0 10 3	2 9 9	17 19 0
67th . . .	3 0 0	0 9 0	2 11 0	15 8 0
68th . . .	3 0 0	0 7 8	2 12 4	12 15 8
69th . . .	3 0 0	0 6 5	2 13 7	10 2 1
70th . . .	3 0 0	0 5 1	2 14 11	7 7 2
71st . . .	3 0 0	0 3 8	2 16 4	4 10 10
72nd . . .	3 0 0	0 2 4	2 17 8	1 13 2
73rd . . .	1 14 0	0 0 10	1 13 2	—

The first table is an estimate of the " Cost in pounds ster-
ling " setting out how the £200 per family would be spent
in the instances of any number of emigrants from five persons to two hundred and fifty thousand persons, and the
sums which they would be called upon to repay at 6 per
cent. (including 1 per cent. sinking fund).

The second is an " approximate Statement showing annual
charges, income and probable surplus ".

The third is an " approximate Statement showing security
for loan ".

These figures are, I think, interesting and suggestive,
although on some points open to criticism. Thus, in the
Annual Charges statement, I am in doubt whether 1 per
cent. is sufficient to allow for management and general improvement expenses; also it remains to be proved whether
money can now be borrowed exactly at 3 per cent., even
with a Government guarantee. If these amounts must be
increased the surplus would be proportionately decreased.
In the same way it might be a wise precaution to halve the
net balance surplus, and in the third table (that showing the
security for loan) to put the value of land after ten years'
colonisation at a lower figure, though it is very probable that,
in fact, it would be higher. Yet when all this is done, the
investment, according to these estimates, still appears to be
sound.

35. As against the transportation expenditure alluded to
above, we must set the fact that, in Canada at any rate, the
land the settlers would occupy is promised as a free gift,
subject only to the provision that the Canada Homestead
Regulations are observed, or whatever slight modification
thereof might be agreed upon to meet the special circumstances. As to this point, although it is obtained for nothing, I may add here that I do not propose that this land
should be handed over free to the settlers, but rather that
a reasonable charge for it should be made against them,
and that the amount thus realised should be used to repay the prime cost of their transportation, a suggestion to
which I daresay the Canadian Government would accede,
and to form a fund for further colonisation and emergency
purposes.

36. To sum up, the utter impossibility at this stage of

giving an exact estimate of the cost of settlements which are not yet fixed upon, does not in any way shake my conviction that where the lands and the markets are good, the people wisely chosen and wisely distributed, and the management is experienced, continuous, and sympathetic, the enterprise can be carried on without loss and very possibly at an actual profit, after allowing for the payment of 5 per cent. interest on money which would be borrowed at about 3 per cent., and an extra 1 per cent. for sinking fund.

37. I would propose that the settlements should not be too small, say not under one hundred families each, since numbers insure plenty of society, which, in the case of persons taken from cities, is, in my opinion, almost a condition of success, especially in a country where the winters are long. Also, I propose that co-operative institutions for the sale and purchase of produce and necessaries should be established in each Land Colony, and with these People's Credit Banks on the well-tested and approved Raffeisen principle that has shown itself to be so successful abroad and, I believe, in Ireland. In this maiden soil both these institutions should flourish greatly, and to the public benefit.

38. A danger that must be guarded against would be that of the creeping in of the land speculator, who might try to buy out the colonist as soon as he saw that his holding was increasing largely in value. This, I think, could be met by giving to the Superintendent of Land Settlements, or to the Salvation Army, or to whatever body the title is vested in until the settler had earned his right to it by the payment of all his liabilities, a power of pre-emption, the amount payable being fixed by independent valuation.

39. The criticism may be advanced that there is no need to go to distant Colonies in order to place such a scheme as I have outlined in operation; that its benefits, at any rate, should not be confined to outlying portions of the Empire, as there is nothing to prevent their application at home.

With such a criticism I am myself in great sympathy. I shall, therefore, be glad, if I am so directed by His Majesty's Government, to prepare a separate memorandum upon the possibility of the establishment of rural Colonies in the United Kingdom, by the aid of the same machinery

2 *

which I have suggested as suitable to the case of their establishment overseas.

40. Before leaving this branch of the subject, for the sake of clearness I will recapitulate the suggestions which I have the honour to advance.   They are :—

(1) That the interest of a loan, or loans, of an amount to be fixed hereafter, should be guaranteed by the Imperial Government, or by the Imperial and certain Colonial Governments jointly, if that is thought desirable and can be arranged.

(2) That the Poor Law Authorities in the large cities of Great Britain should be approached in order to ascertain whether they would be prepared to make a *per capita* contribution for every selected family of which the burden was taken off the local rates.

(3) That a permanent officer should be appointed by the Imperial Government, to be known as the Superintendent of Land Settlements, whose duties and responsibilities I have sketched out above.

(4) That the Salvation Army, or any other well-established and approved social, charitable, or religious Organisation, should be deputed to carry out the work of selecting, distributing, and organising the settlers on Land Colonies anywhere within the boundaries of the British Empire, who should remain in charge of such Organisation until all liabilities were paid.

(5) That no title to land should be given to any colonist until he had discharged these liabilities, on which he should pay 5 per cent. interest and 1 per cent. sinking fund, recoverable in an agreed period of years.

(6) That the possibility of establishing similar Colonies in the United Kingdom should be carefully considered.

(7) That, if these suggestions are approved, a Bill, to be designated the "National Land Settlements Act," embodying and giving life to them, should be laid before Parliament.

41. Before I close this report perhaps I may be allowed to state my general conclusions upon the questions with which it deals.

For a good many years I have studied this matter closely in all its bearings, and, as time goes by, my conviction is strengthened that there is but one cure for certain of the evils which our civilisation has brought with it; to get behind them, to dam them at their source. The wretchedness of our overcrowded cities, indeed, may be beyond any complete remedy, but it can, at least, be palliated by bringing numbers of their poor inhabitants into contact with the healthful plenty of the land.

Some say, however, that even such palliation is impossible, for the reason that the dwellers in cities, or those who purpose to dwell in them, desire to have nothing to do with the land, and refuse to live thereon.

This has never been my experience; in fact, every year considerable numbers of persons write to me individually asking me to help them to convey themselves and their families back from the towns to the country. I believe that in a majority of cases village-born folk go to cities, and in many instances remain in them, because they can find no opportunity or prospect upon the land and, subsequently, because they have not the means to escape with their wives and children from the web of town life in which they have entangled themselves. Given that prospect and opportunity, and given those means, such folk will avail themselves of them with eagerness.

42. These are the views in which my recent investigations confirm me, and I think that much support of them will be found in the individual statements made by the Colonists of Fort Romie and Fort Amity. I believe that in our great cities there exists tens of thousands of persons qualified to make good settlers who would rejoice in an opportunity of escaping from the poverty, sickness, and vices of such places, and with their families, of establishing themselves under healthful conditions upon the land, either in Britain or in her Colonies, with the prospect of obtaining there an independence for themselves and health and plenty for their children.

43. If, in the face of the facts which I have adduced, my

opinions are still thought visionary or optimistic, I can only
point out that, speaking broadly, I am delighted to find
them shared by such men as Mr. Roosevelt, the enlightened
and far-seeing President of the United States, whom, if I
may venture to say so, I thought one of the clearest visioned
and most able statesmen that ever I had the honour of
meeting; by the Honourable Mr. Wilson, who was born
a Scotchman, but is the Secretary for Agriculture in the
same country, a man of vast experience; by Earl Grey, the
Governor-General of Canada, who knows so much of colonisation and its possibilities, and with whom I had many
conferences upon this subject; by General Booth, of the
Salvation Army, whom I saw before leaving England, who,
perhaps, is better acquainted with the actual conditions of
our poor than any other living man, who, moreover, is the
author of practical experiments in land settlement in many
climes, and by others of equal ability and weight. If my
views are visionary, then all of us suffer from similar
delusions.

44. I venture to submit, however, for your consideration
and that of His Majesty's Government that they are sound.
I will go further even, and state my profound conviction
that the future welfare of this country, and, indeed, of others
which might be named, among them the United States,
depends upon whether or no it is possible to retain or to
settle upon the soil a fair proportion of its, or their, inhabitants. Upon that soil men and women grow up in
health, and become furnished with those sober and enduring
qualities which have made the greatness of our nation in
the past, who, if they are relegated to the unwholesome
conditions and crowded quarters of vast cities, must dwindle
in body and change in mind.

45. Nor is this all, since in these cities, as statistics and
experience prove alike, the families are smaller than those
that are born upon the land. Children there are called, and,
indeed, often are, "encumbrances". More of them die in
infancy also, and of those who grow up, many, at any rate
in the second generation, are of a stuff so different that
except for the accident of their common speech they might
well be supposed to belong to another race.

How is it possible, indeed, that children should be born

in adequate numbers, or, if born, thrive, in the crowded slums of London or in the tenement houses of New York, and how can that people remain great and powerful whose supply of healthy children is curtailed? If these are lacking, all the merchandise of the seas and all the treasures of the earth will not supply their place.

46. Therefore, if the future safety of their countries is to be made secure against obvious and disastrous contingencies, in my humble judgment one of the chief aims of the Governments of the highly civilised white nations should be to keep population upon the land; to multiply the numbers of those modest rural homes where men and women desire offspring for their own sakes, and to share their labours and their plenty.

This, it seems to me, can best be done by turning to practical account the public Credit and the waste forces of Benevolence; by using these powers to counteract, at least to some extent, that tendency towards race-ruin, a product of our western culture, whereof the end must be a progressive national weakening and depletion which, if unchecked, may well bring about national defeat at the hands of those ruder peoples of the World that remain land-dwelling and agricultural, and again, as in past ages, culminate in national despair and death.

47. Finally, I suggest that notwithstanding the miscalculations which have been made there, the instances of Fort Romie and Fort Amity do point out a road which may lead to successful colonisation upon a large scale. Again I would repeat, however, that if this is to succeed, there are three essential conditions which must be recognised:—

Sufficient capital, obtained at a moderate rate of interest:

Careful selection of the settlers and of the land:

Skilled and sympathetic management of both after settlement.

48. It cannot be too clearly understood that neglect of any of these requisites, and especially the want of a proper system of finance, will almost certainly end in failure; whereas if they are strictly adhered to, I believe that success can be made very probable, if not absolutely assured.

49. I have omitted to state that I have carefully considered the nature of the tenure which could be given to

land settlers with most advantage to themselves and the greatest security to the Authorities guaranteeing the Settlement Loan. There is no doubt that in some ways the system of perpetual leasehold at a fixed rent is attractive, especially if it could be coupled with a right to buy, since then the colonist is not burdened with the necessity of paying the purchase price of the land, but has only to discharge an annual rent.

50. In countries where land is very costly this plan, therefore, would be worthy of consideration, as under it all the settler's borrowed capital can be expended upon his live and dead stock. In other countries, however, where land is cheap the argument in favour of leasehold is not so strong, while in Canada I am not sure that it would be allowed.

51. My conclusion is that on the whole I agree with the view expressed by Mr. Secretary Wilson and give my voice in favour of freehold, wherever it is possible to grant that boon.

52. That great investigator of agricultural conditions, Arthur Young, wrote one hundred and thirty years ago of the " magic of property ". What he said then holds true to-day. Perpetual leasehold may be virtually as good as a freehold and cheaper to acquire, but sentiment must be taken into account, and considered from this point of view, it does not look the same. The man who starts out to work a piece of land would like to know that a time must come when he will be able to call it his very own. It is because this is impossible that thousands of those who are employed in English agriculture are now deserting the country for the towns. Without the prospect of ownership, or, at the least, of becoming farmers on their own account, they will not stay upon the land.

53. I think, therefore, that the title given to all settlers, at any rate in the British Colonies, after they have discharged their liabilities and paid the price of the land they occupy, should be freehold and no other.

54. Perhaps I may be allowed to suggest that it would be desirable for His Majesty's Government to send a Commissioner to South Africa, with instructions to inquire into the suitability of that country for land Settlements, the terms upon which lands can be acquired for that purpose,

and whether or no any of the South African Governments are prepared to assist in the matter.

55. It has occurred to me that many would-be settlers from Great Britain might think that the climate of Canada is too cold for them, and desire to emigrate to a warmer country. From my general knowledge of South Africa, where I have myself farmed in bygone years, and from what Earl Grey, Sir Marshal Clarke, and others tell me of Rhodesia, I am inclined to think that there is a land whereon settlers might be placed to their own great benefit, and to that of the Empire.

56. So far as I can learn and judge it is becoming more and more evident that the future of Rhodesia is largely agricultural, and now when it has been discovered that, amongst other crops, tobacco of the best possible quality can be grown there, parts of this territory seem to me to offer opportunities for the " small holder ". More than this I cannot say, as I have not had the advantage of recent personal investigation.

57. I append among the other documents, some Remarks upon the Hadleigh Colony of the Salvation Army in Essex, for the reason that the place might prove useful as a training ground for the managers of Settlements, or of industries, such as brick-making and carpentering, which will be practised in them. I thoroughly inspected this Colony before leaving England, and was much interested and impressed by what I saw there.

58. I have to thank His Excellency Sir Mortimer Durand, His Majesty's Ambassador to the United States ; Sir P. Sanderson, His Majesty's Consul-General at New York ; President Roosevelt ; Mr. Secretary of State Hay ; Mr. Secretary Paul Morton ; Mr. Secretary Wilson ; Mr. Under-Secretary of State Loomis, all of the United States Government ; Commissioner Henry Macfarland, and many others for their great kindness towards me, and the assistance which they gave to me, both in my official and my personal capacity.

I have also to thank the Chambers of Commerce and other municipal Bodies and the Clubs in various cities of the United States which I visited, for the many public receptions and hospitalities which they extended or offered to me.

I have to thank Doctor Wheeler, President of the University of California at Berkeley, for his courtesy in inviting me to visit that great institution, where I had the honour of addressing an audience of over three thousand students and others.

I have to thank the President, Counsellors and Apostles of the Mormon Church for their reception of me at Salt Lake City, and the information which they gave me there.

I have to thank Sir Wilfrid Laurier, Premier of the Canadian Government, and other Ministers of that Government, also the Honourable Mr. Sifton, for the patience and the attention with which they listened to my arguments and investigated the evidence that I laid before them with reference to the objects of my mission.

Most of all I have to thank His Excellency Earl Grey, Governor-General of Canada, for his wise counsel and the assistance he afforded me in every way, and on every occasion. Had it not been for that counsel and assistance it would not, I think, have been possible for me to attain the results set out in this report. Such success as those results may be held to represent is due, therefore, to Earl Grey rather than to myself.

I have to thank the citizens of Toronto and Ottawa for the great kindness and cordiality of their welcome towards me. I shall always remember with pride the occasions on which they entertained me at their respective cities when I had the honour of addressing many hundreds of their leading men.

My gratitude is due to Miss Evangeline Booth and many other Officers of the Salvation Army in the United States and Canada for much help which they gave me, and especially to Mr. Ranson Caygill, Treasurer of the Industrial Homes Company of the Salvation Army, and to his assistant, Mr. Harry A. Wright, who were deputed by the Army Authorities to accompany me upon my journey round America. Without their help the difficulties and fatigues of that journey would have been enormously increased.

It is due also to my daughter, Miss Angela Rider Haggard, who acted as my private secretary throughout my mission, and was of great assistance to me.

Further, as one interested in this work for its own sake,

and in all that tends to counteract the grave social and national ills with which it is concerned, perhaps I may be allowed to offer my earnest thanks to the Rhodes Trustees, to whose initiative this inquiry owes its origin and financial support.

59. I thought that it would be more satisfactory to all concerned that there should be an independent sworn valuation of the lands, crop and stock of the two principal Salvation Army Colonies in the United States. It will be seen that these have been furnished, also that the correctness of the figures and statistics handed to me, has, at my request, been verified by oath.

60. I send herewith some photographs [1] of the Colonies of Fort Romie and Fort Amity and their inhabitants, although I do not know whether it is feasible to reproduce them in a Blue-book.

61. Trusting that I may be held to have fulfilled my instructions to your satisfaction and to that of His Majesty's Government, also that the suggestions which I have ventured to advance may prove of service,

I am, Sir,

Your Most Obedient, Humble Servant,

H. RIDER HAGGARD,

Commissioner.

To the Right Honourable
   The Secretary of State for the Colonies.
      5th May, 1905.

[1] Not reproduced in Blue-book.

No. 3.

Washington, D.C.

(These Notes have been submitted to and approved by Mr. Wilson.)

On the 8th of March, 1905, I had the advantage of a long interview with the Honourable James Wilson, Secretary of Agriculture for the United States, a gentleman of the very greatest ability and most extended experience. In the course of this meeting I talked over with him confidentially various aspects of the question upon which I am reporting, and especially those which have to do with the possibility of settling persons who have recently migrated or are about to migrate from the country to the town. It was with real satisfaction that I found Mr. Wilson's and my own views to be practically identical.

After I had outlined my ideas to him, he informed me that in his opinion, if executed upon a foundation of sufficient capital and proper management, there could scarcely fail to be success, provided that the settlers chosen were industrious and willing to overcome certain inevitable difficulties ; provided also that the cost of the land settled was moderate, and that access to markets was easy. He agreed with me that it would be advisable to make a start with people who from early associations, or otherwise, had some idea of farm work, although they need not necessarily be farmers ; that is to say, individuals who had not long been denizens of a great city. He added that when the scheme had got into full swing it would be easier to deal with " green hands ".

Mr. Wilson said that to him it appeared very sad to see so many of our English people flocking from the land to the cities, and that he quite appreciated the disastrous results and the national difficulties that must arise from a continuance of this state of things.

He informed me that in the United States much has been done during the last eight years to benefit farmers by the institution of a good service of mail delivery and in other ways. He remarked also (and this is a curious circumstance) that the establishment of the telephone in every house had done a great deal to keep people on the land, as it helped to destroy the sense of isolation and loneliness, and generally to make life more convenient and interesting. Thus he pointed out that after a day's work the women could gossip with each other over miles of wire, who in former days might perhaps rarely see a visitor.

I asked him what in his opinion would be the best form of tenure to give to such settlers, perpetual leasehold or freehold. He declared himself unhesitatingly to be in favour of freehold, with which, in his opinion, no leasehold, however long and attractive, could possibly compete in the eyes of intending settlers. The prospect of acquiring a freehold, he said, would give the colonist something to work for; some object to be gained beyond that of earning his daily bread. He was sure that if absolute ownership of the land occupied by such settlers could be assured to them within a reasonable period, it would prove a great incentive to exertion.

I pointed out to him the danger that such settlers might be tempted to sell their interests to speculators. He considered my fears upon this point to be exaggerated, adding that in the United States few speculators wished actually to buy out the proprietors of land. Although occasionally they would lend them money rather than take possession, however, as a rule, they renewed the loan. Even Indians, he said, were now allowed to acquire freeholds and to deal with them as they chose. Nor had bad results ensued, although, compared to white men, Indians were as children and were more difficult to manage than any class of folk who would be likely to come under the provision of a settlement scheme.

I asked Mr. Wilson whether he approved of a suggestion I made that the land should be paid for by instalments, calculated to include satisfaction of the interest on the loan and a sufficient sinking fund to discharge the money advanced in the purchase of the land in a period of about thirty-three years. He replied that he approved of that period, but was of opinion that the payments should be made annually and not semi-annually. He believed that in most cases, if the settlements were formed under advantageous conditions as regards to cost of land, locality, etc., it would be found that the settlers would, however, pay off all obligations in a much shorter period than thirty-three years.

In short, I could discover no point of difference between

Mr. Wilson's views and my own.   I may add that he agreed
with me that it would be quite necessary that charitable
bodies who undertook the selection of Colonists and the
management of settlements should be under the control of
a Government official, where the Government is interested,
who could check extravagance, mismanagement, or undue
pressure of any sort.   He agreed also that such settlements
where the Government is not interested would be far better
and more cheaply directed by charitable bodies than by a
number of expensive Government officials.

H. RIDER HAGGARD.

No. 4.

Government House,
Ottawa, 13th April, 1905.

SIR,

I HAVE the honour to inform you that I have been appointed by His Majesty's Government, a Commissioner to investigate certain land settlements in the United States, and should my opinion thereon be favourable, to proceed to Canada and to consult with His Excellency Lord Grey and his Ministers upon the matter generally.

My opinion as to these land settlements being, upon the whole, favourable, I now venture to ask you confidentially whether the Government of the Dominion is prepared to donate a tract of suitable land, to be selected by myself or other Commissioners appointed by His Majesty's Government, for the purpose of the settlement of carefully selected families, taken from among the poor of Great Britain, let us say, a tract of 240,000 acres, or ten townships.

I ask this question under the supposition that sufficient funds for such settlement can be provided under the auspices of the British Government, and that the selection of the settlers and the future management of the settlement can be provided for in a satisfactory and business-like manner.

At the present stage I do not trouble you with details, but I shall be happy to meet you and give you any further information that you may require.

I feel it my duty to make it clear to you that this communication is confidential, and written entirely upon my own responsibility, although I am not without hope that should your answer be in the affirmative, its results might prove both useful and important.

I shall have to leave Ottawa on Monday next, at the latest, and I, therefore, make bold to ask that this letter may receive your present consideration. I need scarcely add that it will strengthen my hands if I am in a position to submit to the Imperial Government some such definite offer of land in Canada as I have outlined above.

I am, etc.,
H. RIDER HAGGARD.

To the Right Honourable
  Sir Wilfrid Laurier, G.C.M.G.,
    etc., etc., etc.

No. 5.

Government House, Ottawa,
13th April, 1905.

MY DEAR SIR WILFRID,

MR. RIDER HAGGARD, who has received instructions from His Majesty's Government to investigate certain land settlements in the United States, and in the event of such settlements affording in his opinion an example which can with advantage be reproduced elsewhere, to consult with me and the Dominion Government as to the opportunities in Canada for the establishment of similar settlements in the Dominion, has arrived here, and has shown me the confidential report he has prepared for Mr. Lyttelton.

I have in accordance with your request introduced Mr. Rider Haggard to Mr. Sifton, and they have had a long talk. Mr. Rider Haggard has also, at my request, shown Mr. Sifton his confidential report.

I have no hesitation in giving expression to my opinion that it is desirable in the interests both of Canada and of the United Kingdom that an effort should be made to apply to some of the unoccupied lands of the Dominion the methods of the settlements which have formed the subject of Mr. Haggard's report.

I have asked Mr. Rider Haggard to write to you the letter which I have the honour to enclose.

Mr. Rider Haggard is unfortunately compelled to leave Ottawa on Monday next, but perhaps it may be possible for you to give me some indication before he leaves as to the character of the co-operation which the Dominion Government may be willing to give to His Majesty's Government in a joint attempt to carry into effect a policy, which, if successful, cannot fail to be a great advantage to the Dominion.

I have asked Mr. Sifton to join the dinner at which you will meet Mr. Rider Haggard to-morrow, Friday, and he has accepted.

I remain, etc.,
GREY.

No. 6.

Prime Minister's Office, Canada, 10th April, 1905.[1]

DEAR SIR,

I HAVE your favour of yesterday. I shall have much pleasure to discuss with you the project as to which you write to me. I regret that at this moment I cannot fix a day or hour for our meeting, but I am going to have the honour of dining with you this evening at Government House, and if then convenient, we will arrange for an interview.

Yours respectfully,
WILFRID LAURIER.

H. Rider Haggard, Esq.,
Government House.

[1] This date should be 14th April, 1905.—H. R. H.

No. 7.

Armadale, Ottawa, 16th April, 1905.

MY DEAR SIR,

I HAVE given a good deal of thought during the last few days to your proposed scheme for placing deserving but impecunious people from the cities of Britain upon farms in Canada, and I am convinced that it offers the promise of success. As you know, I have expressed a favourable opinion to Sir Wilfrid Laurier, and I am pleased to know that he has given a satisfactory assurance of support on the part of his Government, by placing the required area of land at your disposal.

Given the land and a practicable system of selection and management, in regard to which you have the co-operation of the Salvation Army, than which no agency can be more efficient, the only thing remaining is the capital.

It has occurred to me that possibly the British authorities might desire to have a small Committee or Board of Trustees, upon whom there would be one person known to have experience in dealing with this subject and familiar with settlement work in Canada. If it should be thought that I can be of any assistance as a member of such a Committee, I should be willing to serve at least for a time.

I sincerely hope that if the matter takes serious shape you will be able to take an active part in the management. No one can carry out such a plan so well as the man who has conceived it and actually tested it by personal observation.

I regard your scheme as an embodiment of the truest and best form of Imperial patriotism, because it is building for the future by helping to give a solid British basis to the population of our Great West.

Wishing you every success,

Believe me, etc.,
CLIFFORD SIFTON.

H. Rider Haggard, Esq.,
Rideau Hall,
Ottawa, Ontario.

No. 8.

Government House, Ottawa,
17th April, 1905.

My DEAR SIR,

I HAVE to acknowledge and heartily to thank you for your letter of yesterday's date.

That, after full consideration, this project generally and my scheme for putting it into active and beneficent operation, should commend itself to a statesman of your experience and knowledge of all the conditions is, to me, another and a very valuable proof of its soundness.

I think your suggestion as to the appointment of a Canadian Committee excellent, and I will, with gratitude, convey to the Imperial Government your offer to serve upon such a Committee.

I thank you very sincerely for the kind expression of your views as regards myself and the future management of the scheme.

I entirely agree with you that if this far-reaching project can be put into active and continuous operation, besides the immediate material benefits that must ensue, both to the settlers and the country in which they settle, it is likely, in the best possible fashion, to advance those objects that all true Imperialists have at heart.

Should the plan go through, I venture to hope that, after reflection, the Government of the Dominion will see its way to assisting in the matter of a guarantee of such portion of the necessary capital as would be expended in Canada. I am sure that if it did so matters would be much facilitated, both in the eyes of the Imperial Government and in those of public opinion at home. Mr. Fielding, whom I had the honour of seeing yesterday, informed me that he intended to discuss this side of the problem with you.

Again thanking you,

Believe me, etc.,
H. RIDER HAGGARD.

To the Hon. Clifford Sifton,
etc., etc.,
Ottawa.

P.S.—I leave Ottawa for New York this afternoon, and sail per *Majestic* Wednesday.

3 *

No. 9.

Prime Minister's Office, Canada, Ottawa,
17th April, 1905.

SIR,

WITH reference to your favour of the 13th instant, I have the authority of His Excellency the Governor-General in Council to inform you that the Government of Canada will be prepared, at any time, to set aside ten townships for the object set forth in your letter.

In the townships so reserved, the policy of the Government will be to give a free homestead to any person selected by yourself or any commissioner appointed by His Majesty's Government, on the sole consideration that the conditions of settlement prescribed by the laws of Canada be complied with.

It should be understood immediately that the school lands and the lands of the Hudson Bay Company will not be subject to entry by the settlers, but will have to be disposed of or acquired according to law.

Should the experiment be successful, I have no doubt that the Government will be disposed to set aside other tracts of lands under similar conditions. The selection of the land will be left altogether to the judgment of the commissioner appointed by His Majesty's Government, but the Canadian Government will deem it their duty to place at the disposal of the commissioner the services of all their agents in the North-West Territories, to assist in the selection of such lands.

The Government of Canada is satisfied that if a proper class of settlers be secured, such a scheme as you have in mind ought to be completely successful, and they venture to hope that you will be allowed to carry it to completion.

Believe me, etc.,

WILFRID LAURIER.

H. Rider Haggard, Esq.,
Ottawa.

No. 10.

Government House, Ottawa,
17th April, 1905.

SIR,

I HAVE the honour to acknowledge the receipt of your despatch of to-day's date.

I thank you and your Government for the most kind consideration, which under the authority of His Excellency the Governor-General in Council, you have been pleased to give to the matters which I have brought before you by letter and in personal conference.

I appreciate to the full the liberality of the offer which you have made, and I will at once lay the same before the Imperial Government.

I am indeed glad to learn that the Government of Canada is satisfied that if a proper class of settlers is secured, such a scheme as I have in my mind ought to be completely successful. I wish to return to them also my sincere personal gratitude for the hope which they express that I may be allowed to carry it to completion.

I regret that I cannot write at greater length, as I should have wished to do, since I am just leaving for New York, in order to sail for England.

I am, etc.,
H. RIDER HAGGARD,
Commissioner.

The Right Honourable
Sir Wilfrid Laurier, G.C.M.G.,
etc., etc., etc.

No. 11.

REMARKS ON THE FORT ROMIE COLONY OF THE SALVATION ARMY IN CALIFORNIA, U.S.A.

1. I arrived at Fort Romie on the 26th of March, and spent the 27th and 28th in investigating that Colony and all the circumstances connected with its origin, progress and population.

2. Fort Romie, that has a gross area of 520 acres, which is shortly to be added to by a further purchase of 170 acres, lies between two ranges of hills, the Gabilan to the east and the Santa Lucia to the west, part of the mountain system known as the Coast Ranges of California. It is situated four miles from the railway station at Soledad, a hamlet on the Southern Pacific Line, distant about 150 miles from San Francisco.

3. The valley between these two ranges of hills is flat in character, and its soil is a beautiful light loam, which appears to average about fifteen feet in depth, that has been washed down from the mountains, and levelled in past ages by the action of the river. As the country here is arid, that is to say, the rainfall is slight and uncertain, the goodness has never been leached or washed out of this soil, which thus retains its primæval fertility. It is so rich that, given a sufficiency of water, the addition of any manure is held to be superfluous; at least crop after crop are taken without this aid. Doubtless, however, a time must come when fertilisers will be necessary, or, in place of them, very deep ploughing.

4. Over the whole area of the Colony are dotted a number of neat wooden cottages, or homesteads, and the view of it surveyed from the western foot-hills is singularly charming in its rural peace. The vivid green of the springing crops, and especially of the Alfalfa, or Lucerne fields, and the numerous grazing cattle and horses, give, moreover, an impression of very considerable agricultural prosperity.

5. The history of the Fort Romie Colony is, in brief, as follows :—

In the year 1898 Commander Booth Tucker, of the Salvation Army, in conjunction with a Committee of the San

CHILDREN AT PLAY, FORT ROMIE.

GENERAL VIEW OF FORT ROMIE.

Francisco Chamber of Commerce, took steps which resulted in the purchase of Fort Romie by the Salvation Army. The exact circumstances connected with this movement will be found in the annexed document, marked 12, which is an attested report of a formal interview between myself and various officers of the Salvation Army, where they are set out in detail.

The land having been purchased at a price of $26,000, or £5,200 sterling, eighteen families drawn from indigent people in San Francisco were settled upon it, in the hope that there they would be able to earn their livelihoods and establish homes.

The result was an utter failure; of those eighteen families but one remains at Fort Romie to-day. The others have all returned to the city, leaving the Salvation Army losers to the extent of $27,000, or about £5,400, most of which was spent in supporting the settlers and in the beginning of a costly system of irrigation.

6. At first sight this fact would seem to crush the life out of any hopes that may have been entertained as to the possibility of settling such folk upon the land, but as a matter of fact in this instance it is capable of a simple and complete explanation. At that time Fort Romie was quite insufficiently and irregularly irrigated; what is known as " dry land," that is soil more or less dependent upon rainfall to support its crops. Now the three years following the introduction of the San Francisco settlers were years of drought. Little could be grown, and like their own stock, the settlers starved, as, under the conditions, I think, they must have starved had they been the most skilled agriculturists in the world. At the least they found husbandry so un-remunerative that they were glad to forsake it, even for the city tenements which they had left.

This serious reverse, therefore, proves nothing as to the possibility or otherwise of settling persons from the towns upon the land; it leaves the whole question very much where it was.

7. Their failure notwithstanding, the authorities of the Salvation Army determined to begin again on new lines. They arranged for the further irrigation of the land with water brought from the Aroya Seco by the Monterey Water

Company, and, at such seasons as this fails, by completing a supplementary system which enables water to be raised from the Salinas River by means of a steam pumping plant, which plant is now the property of the Colonists.

8. Then they selected more settlers, practically destitute men most of them, but persons accustomed to the land, being generally somewhat of the same class as our British agricultural labourers. To these men the land was sold under contract at $100, or £20 sterling, the acre, plus the cost of any improvements, such as buildings, that might exist upon each twenty-acre lot.

9. This purchase-money was made payable in equal annual instalments, spread over a period of twenty years, to which was added interest on deferred payments at the rate of 5 per cent. Further, chattels, such as horses, stock, implements, etc., were sold to the colonists upon a five-year system, under which the price of them was payable in equal annual instalments, to which is added interest upon all unpaid balances at the rate of 6 per cent. per annum.

10. To guard itself against loss also, the Army took a mortgage or some analogous security, over all live and dead stock thus provided. It was further agreed that no title should be given to the land until all payments were completed, and that any settler who neglected to fulfil his obligations could be ejected after notice, and his land and all upon it seized to satisfy his debt.

11. Such are the circumstances and conditions under which the second settlement of Fort Romie was effected about four years ago. I will now sum up the results as they appear to me to-day. Not to mince matters, the experiment has proved a great success. It is true, although a quarter of it is now owing, that, in most instances, but a small proportion of the price of the land has as yet been paid by its purchasers.

12. For this, however, the reason is that the authorities of the Salvation Army have thought it more expedient and advantageous to all concerned to allow the instalments to stand (of course, subject to the 5 per cent. interest), whereby the colonists are enabled to invest the amount of them in the purchase of stock and generally in improving their condition, than to demand payment upon the specified dates.

The truth is that they have no cause for anxiety. The value of their security is increasing yearly, as will be seen by the annexed documents and valuations. Also should any one of the settlers die or elect to leave, or wish to sell, his "equity," that is the balance of what he owns after satisfying all his debt to the Salvation Army and others, would fetch more than the sum total of his obligations.

Indeed, this was admitted to me by several of the men themselves, as may be seen by reference to the brief summaries of conversations I had with them, that I append hereto.

13. These conversations also will give some idea of the remarkable contentment and, indeed, of the gratitude which I have found characteristic of the settlers on Fort Romie. "I praise the Lord every day of my life that we had the chance to come here," said one woman to me, and, in varying degrees, that seemed to be the spirit of them all. Nor is this wonderful when it is remembered that these folk, nearly every one of them, who a few years ago were in the position of day labourers, are now for the most part on the highway to considerable prosperity, and already possess happy homes, healthy families, pleasant surroundings and a sufficiency upon which to live.

14. With three or four exceptions of individuals, who for some reason or other were absent from the Colony, but who, I have ascertained, are all doing well, I personally interviewed every settler, most of them upon their farms. I am, therefore, in a position to state that such is their fortunate case; not from one of them did I hear a single grumble. Further, I visited the school, and there saw their fifty or sixty children, all of them well-fed, well-clothed and full of health.

15. It comes to this, therefore, that it would be difficult to find a better instance of the advantage of skilfully managed land settlement for the benefit of persons without capital than that which is offered by Fort Romie, in California. Indeed, I doubt if such another one exists.

16. It is, however, easy to foresee that in the future certain difficulties may arise. Thus, when the Salvation Army claims are all paid off, as I believe they will be, and the colonists stand upon their own feet, a salutary and

gentle guiding influence will, of necessity, be more or less withdrawn from them. Also with prosperity will come the desire for more land, and, at present at any rate, but little more land is available, although already some of the settlers are hiring summer grazing runs upon the hills. Also as their children grow up they will want farms, and be unable to get them. These are points, however, which can be faced when they arise. Meanwhile the latter two of them suggest that, where it is possible, there should be spare ground around such settlements which can be taken up when it is needed.

17. The lesson to be learned from this example is, that given first-class and accessible land with really good facilities for irrigation, and given the Salvation Army, or some similar Body, to manage it, from charitable motives and not for profit; given, too, sufficient capital and trained discretion on the part of the managers, the settlement of persons of the class of the present colonists at Fort Romie can be carried on indefinitely with an excellent prospect of success.

18. As well might be expected, the extraordinary advantages that such a system offers to people with no capital beyond their hands and their families have already become noised abroad, with the result that for any vacant lot the Salvation Army is overwhelmed by scores of applications. It would seem, indeed, as though, had they the money and the will, they could at once easily find sufficient folk in the United States alone to settle another ten or twenty thousand acres.

19. To argue, however, from this instance that all settlements everywhere must prove equally successful would be very dangerous.

20. To begin with, in the United States, if it can be delivered on them at reasonable rates, the markets for produce are generally excellent, although here also railways charge high, and commission agents are often exorbitant. Again, as was shown by the fate of the unlucky settlers from San Francisco, water must be available in plenty, either in the shape of an assured rainfall, which has the advantage over irrigation that it costs nothing, or in that of irrigation, which has the advantage over rainfall that it can always be turned on when wanted.

Still, there are doubtless many places within the borders

of the British Empire where all these conditions can be
fulfilled.

21. Here I should state that, as is always the case where
"small holders" abound, co-operation is beginning to get a
hold in Fort Romie. Thus, on the future town-site, about
200 yards from the irrigation canal, a large co-operative store
has been established, whereof the profits are divided among
the members on the usual principle.

22. I visited this store and saw Mr. Vanderburg, the
manager, who was formerly State Senator of Oregon. He
informed me that it was doing well and was already supported by most of the colonists. Attached to it is a butcher's
shop, where meat grazed upon the colony is sold. Also
there were cases of eggs which had been taken in exchange
for groceries, etc., and are traded off to San Francisco. This
store was only opened on the 24th of May, 1904, since which
time the volume of its business has doubled. It is now, I
understand, in a position to pay a dividend of between 5
and 10 per cent.

23. Perhaps I should add that I ascertained that the
Salvation Army places no religious pressure upon the colonists
and enforces no religious tests. If the settlers or their
families choose to attend the Army meetings, of course its
Authorities are glad, otherwise they are not pressed so to do.

Various religious denominations appear to be represented
in the community, which includes Protestants of sundry
sects, and also members of the Roman Catholic Faith. But
whilst it refrains from active spiritual interference, the efforts
of the representatives of the Salvation Army are devoted
to the promotion of brotherly kindness in every shape and to
the fostering of an atmosphere of mutual support and help.

24. In conclusion, from the sworn figures furnished and
the statements made to me, it appears that the present
financial condition of the Fort Romie Colony is as follows:
The Salvation Army incurred a loss upon the first settlement
of about $27,000, or £5,400, while the second settlement
shows them to have a surplus in their favour of about
$6,000, or £1,200.

The colonists have an "equity," that is, a surplus of
assets over all liabilities, of above $41,000, or about £8,300,
that is an average of something over $2,000, or £400 each.

The Salvation Army has expended "for the purchase of land and for the establishment and maintenance of the Colony" $64,000, or about £12,500, to which must be added the loss incurred in the first abortive settlement of $27,000, or £5,400, say, nearly £18,000 in all.

Per contra the values of land, improvements, live stock, outfit, etc., is appraised at $113,280, or nearly £23,000, most of which increment, however, goes to the colonists.

25. Under these circumstances I am of opinion that the settlers should have been charged a somewhat higher price for their land; sufficient indeed to allow a margin for incidental and unforeseen expenses (which must otherwise be written off as a loss), and yet leave to them a good profit. What this exact price should be can only be determined by experience, and the individual circumstances surrounding each Settlement.

H. RIDER HAGGARD,
Commissioner.

No. 12.

NOTES OF AN INTERVIEW BETWEEN COMMISSIONER H. RIDER HAGGARD AND VARIOUS OFFICERS OF THE SALVATION ARMY.

The questions were put by the Commissioner, and unless otherwise specified, the answers were given by Colonel Holland.

The Fort Romie Colony,
27th March, 1905.

Before starting to inspect the Colony, the following conversation took place. The names of the persons present are as follows, *viz.*, Colonel Thomas Holland, Staff-Captain Hamon, Colonel French, Mr. R. Caygill (the Commissioner's Secretary), Staff-Captain Erickson, Staff-Captain Wright (the Commissioner's stenographer), and Miss Angela R. Haggard (the Commissioner's Private Secretary).

Q. In what year was the Colony started?

A. In the spring of 1898.

Q. What is the acreage?

A. 520 acres gross, including roads and waterways.

Q. Whom did you buy it from?

A. Mr. Charles Romie.

Q. Was he a farmer here?

A. No; not an actual farmer, but a prominent landowner in this district.

Q. Was it unimproved then?

A. No; it had been farmed as a dry farm up to the time of our purchase, and had three ranches on it.

Q. What price was paid for it?

A. $26,000 for the whole thing (say £5,200).

Q. Was that money left on mortgage?

A. A small amount was paid down at the time, the balance was left on mortgage, but this balance has since been liquidated. Except for the Salvation Army's private financial arrangements with its bondholders, which in varying degree affect all our business interests in the United States, the land is clear.

Q. Just give me your history of this Colony briefly; the system which has been followed, the people you have got; your failures and situation generally.

A. Just prior to the establishment of this Colony or any of our Colonies in the United States, this country was in a very demoralised condition, in consequence of business depression. As a means of relief, Commander Booth Tucker propounded his "landless man to the manless land" proposition, the essence of his plan being summed up in the following manner, viz.: "put the waste labour on the waste land by means of the waste capital, and thus convert this trinity of waste into a unity of production".

At the request of the San Francisco Chamber of Commerce he, Commander Booth Tucker, explained his plan to the members thereof, who were so impressed with its practicability that they appointed a committee of co-operation to assist the Salvation Army in the establishment of a Colony in this State of California. As a result of the joint endeavours of Commander Booth Tucker and the Chamber of Commerce Committee, a small beginning was made in the Salinas Valley on the land referred to as above, and now known as Fort Romie.

Unfortunately for the parties interested and the scheme, the beginning was made just on the threshold of a drought, which lasted for three years, and which devastated agricultural conditions throughout the arid portion of the State. In the general loss and disappointment which this entailed, we were very unfortunate participators. The question will naturally arise in your mind as to whether we should suffer similarly in the event of another drought presenting itself. To this I would say that our facilities for irrigating have since then been so perfected as to practically safeguard us against any such contingency.

We started with eighteen pioneer families—a total of about seventy-five souls—all drawn from city folk, and most of whom were "out-of-works". Because of conditions arising from the drought they really did not have a fighting chance, and not knowing how long that state of affairs would last they gave up their allotments and returned to the city. I must impress upon you, however, Mr. Commissioner, that these conditions were absolutely abnormal, since, even if such a drought should recur, we are now able to meet it with improved water facilities.

Q. Supposing the seasons had been normal and you had had at that time your present water supply, do you think those families would have failed and have departed?

A. I see no reason why they should not have succeeded and done nearly as well as the colonists who followed them. The start of our Colonisation Scheme, as it now appears, really dates, therefore, with the present batch of settlers, the most of whom came in the spring of 1901.

Q. Who were those men—I mean to what class did they belong?

A. With one or two exceptions, they were all poor men living in this district, and their position was somewhat analogous to that of the British agricultural labourer. In almost every instance they were men without capital. We selected them because they were farmers by profession and thoroughly understood the peculiar conditions to which they were subject. The high price of the land and the difficulties attendant upon the development of our water supply were such as made us feel that such a type of man as I have described was necessary to the successful operation of the Colony.

In this respect Fort Romie differs from Fort Amity, whose colonists were largely drawn from the cities and were in every case men without capital.

The present number of colonists comprises twenty families, holding an average of twenty acres each. No colonist accepted since 1901 has left the Colony. There were two families who came in with the intention of becoming colonists, but they withdrew again without putting in a crop, and one other man left in consequence of serious ill-health, which rendered the climate unsuitable to him.

What these colonists have done will, of course, be shown by their individual balance sheets, which have been prepared for your inspection, and on appraisements made by two independent and disinterested valuators and properly certified. From these you will observe that the amount of money paid in on their accounts by the colonists is comparatively small. We have not worried about this, however, because we found that these people, starting without capital, had to spend what money their farms would produce in the purchase

of cattle, implements, etc., and in the improving of their
lands and buildings, so as to warrant the prospect of their
being able to do better as a result. The balance sheets referred to show that most of the colonists have a very
gratifying "equity" in their property. By "equity" I mean
the difference between their property in the land, with the
stock, crops, buildings and outfit, and the amount which
they owe to the Salvation Army or to any other creditor.

Q. That is satisfactory as far as it goes, but I want you
to explain to me what is the exact system under which
these men are located on the land; what are their obligations and their rights, and is the Colony run as a business
proposition, from which the Salvation Army expects to
make no loss, if, indeed, it does not make a profit, or is it
run as a charity?

A. The land was sold to colonists under contract at $100
per acre, to which was added any cost of improvements
upon the land in the shape of buildings, this amount to
be paid in equal annual instalments, spread over a period
of twenty years, with interest at 5 per cent. on deferred
payments. Chattels, consisting of cows, horses, implements,
waggons, etc., are sold on a five-year instalment plan, payable
in equal annual instalments, instalments being spread over
each year equally, and with interest on all unpaid balances
at the rate of 6 per cent. per annum. In selling movable
chattels of this description, we insure ourselves against loss
by taking a mortgage upon the animals and articles sold.

Q. Have you ever had any occasion to foreclose one of
these mortgages?

A. No; never on this Colony.

Subject to the discharge of their duty towards the Salvation Army, the colonists are as much freeholders as any
other persons who have purchased estates, but should they
fail to fulfil those obligations, they can, after due notice
being given, be dispossessed, and the land, and all they
have on it, be taken to satisfy their debt.

As regards the last part of your question, Mr. Commissioner, I answer, that the Colony is certainly run as a
business proposition by the Salvation Army, and not as a
charity. The Army does not expect, and cannot afford,
to make losses upon these schemes, which are undertaken

by the Salvation Army in a spirit of philanthropy, it is
true, but with the object of inculcating the principles of
self-support by assisting indigent persons to become owners
of homes and lands, and independent and self-supporting
citizens.

Q. Well, Colonel, after these years of experience, how far
do you consider those objects have been attained on Fort
Romie.

A. I should add that, speaking broadly, none of the ex-
penses of management are borne by the colonists or the
Colonies.   These are given to the scheme by the Salvation
Army as a part of their philanthropic work.

Q. I quite understand, but I should like you to tell me
what, upon another basis, namely, that of the ordinary
remuneration paid to managers of land in this country, would
the charges of running this Colony actually amount to per
annum.

A. Say $2,000 (about £400 per annum), to which must
be added small incidental expenses, say another $500.   Of
course, however, you must understand that our scale of
payments to our own people are not based upon those of the
current wages of those countries in which they may happen
to be serving, but upon what is considered sufficient for their
mere support in the work in which they may be engaged.
Thus, in the case of the Fort Romie Colony, the Manager's
remuneration does not exceed half the amount I have
mentioned, out of which he has to support his wife and
family.

Q. With reference to the question I put to you just now,
have you now any fears of the Colony as a business proposition?

A. No, Sir; the land has been so improved by settlement
and its value so increased by the irrigation works that we
have constructed, that what we purchased at $50 per acre
could now be readily sold at from $100 to $150 per acre, in
accordance with its position and improvements.

Q. (The Commissioner to the Manager, Staff-Captain
Erickson) : Does your opinion coincide with that of Colonel
Holland?

A. Yes; most fully.

Q. (The Commissioner to the company assembled) : Have

4

any of you other gentlemen anything to take exception to in the evidence which has been given, or to add to it?

A. Staff-Captain Hamon: I think it could be supplemented by saying that we have acquired here in this effort and example a valuable fund of experience, which will stand us in good stead on a larger scale in other states or countries. For colonist purposes, that is with the object in view of assisting the poor man to become the owner of a home upon the land, I do not consider it a good plan for the Army to acquire high-priced land. If the Army does so it will assuredly heap upon the colonist a burden almost too heavy for him to bear. In my opinion, cheaper land, if good, such as can be obtained in many parts of the world, would serve our purposes just as well, and in some ways much better.

A. Staff-Captain Erickson: A man with previous farming experience is far more desirable as a colonist than one without it.

Q. Do you mean by that it is your opinion that this principle cannot be applied to any persons taken from towns, even although they may have originally come from the land?

A. Staff-Captain Erickson: No; what I mean to say is this, that a person with some farming experience, or some connection with the land, is better qualified as a colonist.

A. Colonel Holland: I agree with Staff-Captain Erickson, that if a man has had prior experience on a farm, that he possesses an advantage over the man without that experience. But it has been proved that men who are so ignorant of farm life as not to know the difference between a plough and a harrow have shown themselves to be amongst our most successful agriculturists.

Q. Where?

A. At Fort Amity, Colorado.

This not only applies to the men, but to their wives and children. In fact, on this line I would like to say that after seven years' experience with this work, I have yet to meet the first person—man, woman, or child—who had been brought on to the Colonies from the city who had any desire to return thereto.

Q. You except, I presume, those colonists who, after a three years' drought, went back from this Colony, Fort Romie, to San Francisco?

A. No, Sir; I do not. They did not return to the city because they were tired of the country, but because the unfortunate abnormal natural conditions already referred to made it impossible for them to remain.

Q. You mean that they were starved out and had to go, whether they liked it or not?

A. Yes; and naturally they went to where they had associations and thought they might find employment.

A. Staff-Captain Hamon: I may add, Mr. Commissioner, that in the settlement of colonists, it does not follow that the operations on a large scale would necessitate putting on poor city people only. Thus, in forming a settlement the poor city men might be located on lots 1, 2, 4, 5 and 6, and on lot 3, in the centre, might be placed the person experienced in agriculture. This system might be pursued until the lesson had been learned by the help and experience gained, and we could deal with city folks in blocks. What is needed in the initial stages of operation are " pace-setters " and examples.

Q. Why did you select such expensive land?

A. The active participation of the Chamber of Commerce, in San Francisco, was with a view to the establishment of a Colony in this State for the benefit of its own citizens. All land in California, capable of irrigation, is high priced, and what we purchased in the Salinas Valley, notwithstanding its high price, was a cheap proposition from a commercial standpoint. The purchase has justified itself by the fact that the land could now be sold at twice the amount of money which we paid for it. At the same time, I quite agree with Staff-Captain Hamon that the colonising of city poor should not be undertaken on high-priced lands, because the large amount of debt that a settler has to face from the start makes his acquirement of a freehold look so far from him that he is apt to get discouraged, and so the obligation is too much for him. Such a condition is the more liable to occur because of the comparatively heavy interest charges that he is forced to meet. Since an abundance of cheap land can be obtained in this and other countries, I am thoroughly at one with Staff-Captain Hamon in his view that future colonisation should be carried out on cheap lands; that is so far as the British Colonies and the United

4 *

States are concerned. If such land were selected in rain-belt districts, it would be so much the better, especially if it were in a timber region, where the cost of building material and fuel would be reduced to the minimum.

A. Staff-Captain Erickson : I cannot quite agree with Colonel Holland's opinion. I feel that there are certain advantages in an irrigated district :—

1. The smaller area required.
2. A closer settlement, and
3. A community of interests which cannot as readily be obtained elsewhere.

Q. Why cannot a community of interest be obtained ?

A. Staff-Captain Erickson : Because irrigation necessitates a certain amount of co-operation among those who avail themselves of it.

A. Staff-Captain Hamon : I think that it is a bad state of affairs if a community of interest does not prevail in every department of such ventures as that under consideration. I consider a community of interests a condition of success, and more particularly so where the area settled is considerable.

Q. You are, all of you, gentlemen of experience in this matter. Is it your opinion that supposing suitable land and sufficient funds are forthcoming to settle the same, that colonists who would make a success of the venture would also be forthcoming in sufficient number, taken from the poor of the English cities, subject, of course, to the condition that such poor were carefully selected and had more or less knowledge of, or connection with, the land ?

A. I should say unhesitatingly, yes, to almost an unlimited extent, and that the result would be the successful settlement of large numbers of people, and to some extent the relieving of the congestion of cities.

N.B.—(The other gentlemen present all agreed with Colonel Holland in his remarks.)

The conversation then came to an end.

H. RIDER HAGGARD,
Commissioner.

THOMAS HOLLAND.
NELS A. ERICKSON.
ALFRED HAMON.

These answers were given to me by Colonel Holland and Staff-Captain Erickson on a subsequent date.

H. RIDER HAGGARD.

8th April, 1905.

STATEMENT made by Colonel THOMAS HOLLAND and Staff-Captain N. A. ERICKSON relative to the Fort Romie Colony.

Q. What is the present financial condition of the Colony?
A. The value of land and improvements, live-stock, outfit, etc., is appraised at $113,280.00.

The Salvation Army has expended for the purchase of land and for the establishment and maintenance of the Colony in round figures $64,000. To this expenditure should be added a loss of approximately $27,000 occasioned by the failure of the plan during the first years; the reasons for this failure being given elsewhere.

Q. Are you solvent?
A. Yes, fully, as regards the present condition of the Colony; if, however, the above-mentioned loss of $27,000 is included, there would be a deficit of approximately $21,000.

The value of land, outfit, etc., still held by the Salvation Army is valued at $18,500; the indebtedness of the colonists to the Salvation Army, including water plant, is $51,654.99. Total $70,154.99.

Q. In the event of sale, would you recover all that you have spent?
A. Yes, with the exception of the loss incurred during the first years.

Q. Would the colonists receive all that they have spent?
A. Yes, and a great deal more.

Q. Would there be anything over, either in the Army's pocket or for the colonists?
A. Decidedly, yes. The colonists hold property appraised at $94,780, on which they owe the Salvation Army and sundry debtors $52,819.20, leaving them an equity of $41,960.80, an average of over $2,000 each.

The Salvation Army assets are sufficient to cover all its expenditure for the Colony (except the loss on the first

year's operations), and leave a surplus of approximately
$6,000.

Q. What did you pay for the land?

A. $26,000.00.

Q. What is its present value with improvements?

A. $95,205.

Q. What would the Colony fetch as a going concern?

A. This question I cannot answer. I assume the value
of the appraisers is correct, and on this basis the Colony,
including land, buildings, improvements, live-stock, equipment, etc., would bring $113,280.

Q. Have you obtained any outside valuation?

A. An appraisement has been made by two competent
and disinterested persons, duly sworn to and submitted
herewith.

THOMAS HOLLAND.
NELS A. ERICKSON.

No. 13.

NOTES OF INTERVIEWS WITH COLONISTS, FORT ROMIE COLONY.

27th and 28th March, 1905.

Equity, $3,311, or about £662.

THOMAS BRYANT :—

A colonist for four years. Had been raising stock; also has a team of horses which he hires out. He pastures his calves on the hills, which he can do for 25 cents per head a month. Has a wife and four children, and was well satisfied with the prospects. He had paid $1,000 on his place to Army, and got home well fixed. Had spent over $500 recently on house, etc.; had twenty-seven head of cattle; reckoned his land, house, cattle, etc., were worth at least $4,000; but he would not take that amount and sell out. He owed the Army $1,800; so an estimate of $4,000 (a price he would not take) showed his " equity " at $2,200. He was well pleased with the Colony, and the system by which he had bought his homestead. He did not suppose he would have ever owned a home or anything had it not been for the Army.

Equity, $859, or about £172.

MR. A. C. CARLE :—

Came to Romie two years ago; was raised on a farm, but was working in a factory before coming to the Colony. He had no capital. On the contrary, he then owed $30. Believed it was a great blessing to him, getting the opportunity of acquiring a home at Romie. He intended to settle permanently on the place. He felt sure he would get on well. Had been raising potatoes and chickens, and intended extending his operations on these lines.

Equity, $879, or about £176.

C. M. HODGES :—

Came here about two years ago. He appeared to be about fifty-five or sixty years of age; beyond the limit, one would imagine, from which colonists should be selected. He

said he had been a schoolmaster, but has also done a little
farming. Did not do particularly well last year, as he had
been a little late in planting his potatoes which were his principal crop. He was sure he was going to do much better
this season. He brought no capital with him to Romie,
though he had a little stock, that, however, had not much
value. He was very glad he had come to Romie ; he preferred
his present position infinitely to working for wages, which he
surely would have been doing had the Army not given him
this opportunity. He had five children—two boys and three
girls.

Equity, $995, or about £199.

MR. C. H. HUME :—

Said he had been at Romie two years, and was farming 20 acres ; had had a little experience in farming before
coming here. Had made no repayments upon land as yet,
but would soon commence doing so. He thought he was
getting on "very fair," and was "well satisfied" that he
had come here. Was going to put 12 acres in potatoes this
year. He believed this would pay as well as anything.
Six tons could be grown from one acre, and the same would
bring from $80 to $90 per acre. He was quite satisfied
with his bargain at Romie, and expected to be able to pay
for his place within five or six years.

Equity, $1,274, or about £255.

MRS. JOHNSON :—

A widow of one of the late colonists; said since her
husband's death she had rented out nine of the twelve acres
constituting her farm. Before her husband came to Romie
he farmed a place he owned on the hills. This she sold
since his death for $2,000. She was getting along very
nicely, indeed. Was renting out the nine acres for $112 per
annum, which more than paid for instalments and interest
due upon the land to the Salvation Army. The remaining
three acres were sufficient for her cow and chicken raising,
which she found very profitable. She appreciated the new
arrangement made with the Army since her husband's death,
which gave her the privilege of staying on the Colony and
bringing up her three fatherless children.

Equity, $1,270, or about £254.

M. EDE HARDING :—

Mr. Harding has been on the Colony six years this winter; before coming here he lived on a "squat" of 160 acres of dry land. He brought no capital with him, excepting a pair of horses, a cow and calf. He now declares himself quite satisfied with his progress. He is the owner of some fifteen cows, which bring him in from $40 to $75 a month. Last month he realised $71 net from ten cows. He considers his property worth $4,000, everything included. He still owes the Army $2,300. Mr. Harding said: "I am glad I came. I could never have got along so well with any one else (referring to the Salvation Army). I don't think there is another company on earth who would have helped me in the same way."

Equity, $2,339, or about £468.

MR. ROBERT MITCHELL :—

Mr. Mitchell had been here four years. He was a Salvation Army Officer, and employed in the printing works at San Francisco; he had also some experience in farming. When he came he had nothing but borrowed money. He stated that he was getting along very well now, but, owing to an accident, had broken his leg, which had been a great drawback to him and lost him a year's work. In the first place he bought everything from the Army, and has paid back some $655. He still owes $2,800, and values his land, stock, etc., at $5,000. Mr. Mitchell said: "I am very glad I came here. I have been with the Army ever since I was 'saved' eight or nine years ago. I did a good day's work when I took this venture. I am satisfied with my prospects; I could not have got such a start if the Army had not been behind me and loaned me the money. I am now in a position to make my payments as they fall due."

Equity, $2,261, or about £452.

MR. C. E. BAETSCHEN :—

A German Swiss, with a family of seven children, was a dairyman, and has been on the Colony four years. He owns a neat house and home, with orchard, containing apple, peach and pear trees in good condition. He has ten cows of Dutch blood, and stated that he is doing well. On his stock he has paid off about $350 to the Army, and he values the whole of his possession at $4,500, and, as near as he can say, still owes $2,700. When he came he had $525 capital, and said as far as he could see this was his only chance of becoming the owner of a home and property, as no one else would push him and give him a chance. Before this he was a hired dairyman in the employ of the Salvation Army.

Mr. Baetschen grinds his corn with the wind machine that pumps his water.

Equity, $6,700, or about £1,340.

MR. M. MATHESON :—

Mr. Matheson is by birth a Dane. He was not at home, but I saw his place which was purchased by him from the Army within two years for $4,650 for 29 acres and the improvements thereon. Previous to this the land had been in the hands of the Salvation Army. The man lived in this neighbourhood, and, therefore, knew the value of land here. He paid for his property outright. We met Mr. Matheson a little later. He stated that he was satisfied with his prospects, and considers the land as good as is to be had; he thinks it will subsequently be worth $400 per acre. He paid $155 per acre for it, and declared he would not take $200 for it to-day.

Mr. Matheson has a family of six children.

Equity, $4,394, or about £879.

MR. LINDSTRAND :—

A Finn by birth, who had a very tidy place, with nice house and pretty little garden, good windmill and cistern, also a small orchard with well-grown trees, and was in the course of erecting a fine wooden barn. He is the sole survivor of the batch of settlers who were starved out by the three years' drought. Originally he was a car conductor in San Francisco. He stated that he had been at Romie nearly eight years, that he had a wife and two children, and held

20 acres of land; that he had lived through the bad time
(the drought) because he "held on," whilst the others went
away too soon.   He had paid off about half of his indebtedness to the Army, and reckoned his house, stock, land and
implements to be worth at least $4,000.   He said that he
still owed $900 to the Army.   Recently he had received
$1,000 left him by a relative, and with this amount he had
paid off his land, etc.   He considered himself a fortunate man
in getting to Romie; he thought he had done very well, and
believed there were brighter prospects for the future.   He
said the new barn which he was putting up would cost him
$300.

NOTE.—I went into Mr. Linstrand's house, which seemed
full of comforts, and contained, among other things, a bicycle
and phonograph.   Also here were stored doors and other
materials to be used in a proposed addition to the dwelling.
—H. R. H.

Equity, $846, or about £169.

MR. A. D. JAMES :—

Stated that he had been at Romie four years.   He
brought no capital, excepting $175.   He wanted a home,
and hearing of this Colony made application.   He had not
much stock, as he was "getting on his feet".   He had
20 acres.   He had not paid anything off his land yet,
but had met instalments due on live stock.   He thought
the value of his stock and land with improvements considerably exceeded the amount of his indebtedness to the Salvation Army.   He had a five-roomed house, which he took
over at a valuation of $300, including a windmill and barn.
Mr. James said he was glad he had come to the Colony, and
he looked forward to making a success of his holding and
was quite satisfied with the arrangement he had made with
the Army.   He had two children at home, who are getting
big enough to be of some help.

Mr. James said, in conclusion, that he would not take
$1,000 for his "equity," that is, if any one were to offer to
pay all his indebtedness to the Salvation Army and give
him $1,000 he would not accept it.

Equity, $1,757, or about £351.

Mr. W. J. Scott:—

Said he came to the Colony four years ago. Previously he had been farming on a small scale, and sometimes working out. He had no capital when he arrived, excepting $30, and a team of two horses. He considers he has been doing "first-rate" at Romie. He has, as yet, paid off no charges on land, but a proportion of his debt on the live stock. He owned thirteen cows, eight calves and fifty-six head of hogs, a span of horses and his crops. He valued the whole lot at $3,500, and he owes the Salvation Army $2,700, and is, therefore, $800 to the good. He was perfectly satisfied with his position and very glad he came to Romie. He had a wife and one boy.

Equity, $3,198, or about £639.

Mrs. Handley:—

Wife of Samuel Handley, who was absent from home, said that her husband had been in the occupation four years, and that they had six children. They farm 20 acres. At first they grew potatoes and beans, but now raise stock. They had in all seventy-four head of cattle, which they fed by renting a place upon the hills in addition to their land upon the Colony. When they came they were without capital, "unless children could be called capital". Also one year they lost almost everything by fire, including their waggon, hay, chickens, etc., etc. They were now getting on "fine". They expected to have land and stock paid for in two years' time, and to be quite clear of debt. Up to the present they had repaid nothing, as all the earnings had gone into the purchase of stock. Mrs. Handley stated, in answer to a question which the Commissioner put to her as to whether she was glad she came to the Colony: "I praise the Lord every day of my life that we had the chance to come here". She added that formerly her husband worked upon the railroad.

Note.—I saw this woman's husband on the following day, and had a long conversation with him. He more than confirmed all her statements.—H. R. H.

Equity, $100, or about £20.

AL. RODDICK said :—

"I have only recently come to the Colony and have taken up 12 acres, upon which I raise chickens. Formerly I worked in the woods. I brought no capital with me. I propose to build a house. I have taken the land upon the ordinary terms, but agree to pay off the cost in twelve years. My land, which is dry land, cannot be irrigated, and on that account is very suitable for chicken raising, is to cost me $38 per acre."

Equity, $2,396, or about £479.

MR. CHARLES HANDLEY :—

Had been on the Colony one year and a half. Occupies house built by the Army, but has improved it. Has four horses, four cows, chickens, etc. Has 20 acres of land, and raises alfalfa and potatoes. Considers he is doing "first-rate". Has a wife and four children. Hopes to pay off all his indebtedness, make a good living, and raise a good stock. Very glad he came to Fort Romie. Previous to coming to the Colony he ran a free farm given by the Government.

Equity, $789, or about £158.

MR. JOHN VRIELING :—

Has 7 acres of land. Been on the Colony about three years, and is doing well. Came from Amity to Romie on account of ill-health. Has 500 chickens. His stock is the white Leghorn. In California the white egg is preferred. Realises from five to six dozen eggs per day.

No. 14.

State of California,
City and County of San Francisco. } SS.

Thomas Holland, being duly sworn, deposes and says: That the price paid for the land comprising what is now known as the "Salvation Army Fort Romie Colony" was twenty-six thousand (26,000) dollars. What sales of this land we have made to colonists amount to thirty-seven thousand, five hundred (37,500) dollars, and we still have upwards of one hundred and thirty (130) acres left, estimated by disinterested and reliable appraisers to be worth twelve thousand (12,000) dollars.

(Signed)   THOMAS HOLLAND.   (L.S.)

Subscribed and sworn to before me this 29th day of March, 1905.

(Signed)   ADELINE COPELAND,
Notary Public in and for the City
and County of San Francisco,
State of California.

No. 15.

State of California,
County of Monterey. } SS.

I, W. H. H. Metz, Supervisor of Monterey County, California, being duly sworn, do hereby depose and state that the attached schedule of property owned by the Salvation Army and the members of the Fort Romie Salvation Army Colony, is a full, true, and correct statement of the property appraised by me this day, and that to the best of my knowledge and belief the values of the property therein given, to wit: ninety-five thousand, two hundred and five dollars for land and improvements, and eighteen thousand and seventy-five dollars for live-stock, farming equipment, and crop, represents the true market value of the property listed.

(Signed)   W. H. H. METZ.

Subscribed and sworn to before me this 29th day of
March, A.D. 1905, at Soledad, in the County of Monterey,
California.

(Signed)   Y. P. VILLEGAS,
Notary Public in and for the
(SEAL.)   County of Monterey, State
of California.

No. 16.

State of California, ⎱ ss.
County of Monterey. ⎰

I, W. H. Bingaman, Real Estate and Insurance Broker,
residing at Soledad, California, being duly sworn, do hereby
depose and state that the attached schedule of property
owned by the Salvation Army and the members of the Fort
Romie Salvation Army Colony, is a full, true, and correct
statement of the property appraised by me this day, and
that to the best of my knowledge and belief the values of
the property therein given, to wit: ninety-five thousand, two
hundred and five dollars for land and improvements, and
eighteen thousand and seventy-five dollars for live-stock,
farming equipment, and crop, represents the true market
value of the property listed.

(Signed)   W. H. BINGAMAN.

Subscribed and sworn to before me this 29th day of
March, A.D. 1905, at Soledad, in the County of Monterey,
California.

(Signed)   Y. P. VILLEGAS,
Notary Public in and for the
(SEAL.)   County of Monterey, State
of California.

No. 17.

Soledad, California, 29th March, 1905.

Property owned by the Salvation Army and the members of the Fort Romie Salvation Army Colony at Fort

Romie, Monterey County, California, with the value thereof as appraised by W. H. H. Metz and W. H. Bingaman.

		$	$
Land :—			
443 acres of irrigated land, including checking and levelling of same, worth at present market prices $145 per acre		64,235	
56 acres non-irrigable land worth $25	.	1,400	
21 acres occupied by canals and roadways.			
Total area 520 acres, valued at		———	65,635
Irrigation system :—			
Plant, including engine, boiler, centrifugal pump, flumes, ditches, water rights, etc.	.	.	6,750
Headgates, stop and checkgates	.	.	400
Trees :—			
Orchard and shade, shrubbery, small fruit, etc.	.	.	3,500
Fencing :—			
About 18 miles boundary and pasture fence valued at $80 per mile, also wire netting	.	1,440	
Pens, corrals, etc..	.	1,000	
		———	2,440
Buildings :—			
22 dwelling houses	.	8,800	
Barns and outbuildings	.	2,000	
Store and office building	.	2,300	
		———	13,100
Water supply :—			
18 wells, 15 windmills, 10 water-tanks, piping, etc.	.	.	3,380
Total value of land and improvements			95,205

	$	$
Live-stock :—		
39 horses and colts	3,000	
128 cows and heifers at $25 each . .	3,200	
155 stock cattle and calves . . .	2,335	
153 hogs	765	
Poultry and bees	425	
		[1] 9,715
Farming equipment :—		
Vehicles and harness	3,000	
Mowers, rakes and haying tools . .	1,500	
Ploughs, harrows, discs, scrapers, seed, drills, and cultivators . . .	1,000	
Cream separators	360	
Troughs, milk cans, irrig. canvas, incubators, tools and sundry equipment .	800	
		6,660
Crop :—		
Hay and crops on hand not harvested . .		1,700
Grand total . .		$113,280

[1] There seems to be an error of ten dollars in this addition. The figures, however, correspond with those of the original document.— H. R. H.

No. 18.

STATEMENT SHOWING THE FINANCIAL POSITION OF THE
COLONISTS, FORT ROMIE COLONY, ON 1st APRIL, 1905,
BASED ON VALUATIONS MADE BY SWORN APPRAISERS.

Name.	Assets.		Liabilities.		Colonists' Equity.
	Land, Buildings and Improvements.	Live Stock, Outfit and Crop.	Due Salvation Army on 1st Oct., 1904.	Other Liabilities.	
	Dollars.	Dollars.	Dollars.	Dollars.	Dollars.
1. T. Bryant . .	4020.00	1300.00	2008.31	—	3311.69
2. E. Harding .	3675.00	1200.00	3087.14	517.00	1270.86
3. Mrs. Johnson .	2600.00	300.00	1625.54	—	1274.46
4. W. G. Boswell .	3420.00	325.00	2796.13	—	948.87
5. S. Handley .	3805.00	2600.00	2641.54	565.00	3198.46
6. O. Lindstrand .	4450.00	900.00	955.76	—	4394.24
7. A. James . .	3650.00	275.00	3047.07	31.00	846.93
8. T. Day . .	3620.00	1725.00	2960.66	400.00	1984.34
9. C. E. Baetschen	3970.00	1350.00	2908.52	150.00	2261.48
10. R. W. Mitchell .	3925.00	1500.00	3035.16	50.00	2339.84
11. W. J. Scott .	3650.00	1500.00	3222.18	170.00	1757.82
12. C. M. Hodges .	3280.00	400.00	2645.98	155.00	879.02
13. C. M. Hume .	3325.00	300.00	2535.06	94.00	995.94
14. D. W. Wiley .	4060.00	—	2229.88	—	1830.12
15. J. F. Nelson .	3550.00	1800.00	2373.77	—	2976.23
16. A. C. Carle .	2360.00	225.00	1628.74	97.00	859.26
17. C. N. Handley .	3635.00	1000.00	2238.87	—	2396.13
18. J. Vrieling .	2410.00	275.00	1860.89	35.00	789.11
19. M. Matheson .	6700.00	—	—	—	6700.00
20. A. Roddick .	450.00	100.00	—	450.00	100.00
Total . . .	70555.00	17075.00	43801.20	2714.00	41114.80

NOTE.—Average equity per colonist, $2055.00, or about £411.

THE SANATORIUM, FORT AMITY.

COLONIST'S COTTAGE, FORT AMITY.

No. 19.

REMARKS ON THE FORT AMITY COLONY OF THE SALVATION ARMY IN COLORADO, UNITED STATES OF AMERICA.

1. I arrived at this Colony on the morning of the 5th April, 1905, and during that and the two following days thoroughly studied its conditions, its inhabitants, their circumstances and methods of farming.

2. Fort Amity is situated on prairie land in the Valley of the Arkansas River, not far from the dividing line between the States of Colorado and Kansas, at an elevation above sea-level of about 3,500 feet. Its area is 1,760 acres, and all the soil is irrigated from the Arkansas River. The climate is extremely healthy, especially for persons with weak lungs, so there is little sickness in the place. In winter it is cold, and in summer rather hot, while in April, just at the commencement of spring, the air is fresh and bracing, and features of the district are the pleasant winds that draw across it, and the intense blueness of the sky.

3. Viewed from the rising ground to the north, Fort Amity consists of a considerable number of dwellings, mostly built of wood, but in some cases of limestone, of a good quality when properly weathered, that is quarried in the neighbourhood. Near to the station, for the Atchison, Topeka, and Santa Fé Railway runs through the Colony, is the town site, where various stores are springing up, which stores, by the way, I am informed last year turned over $200,000, or £40,000, and paid to the railway $50,000, or £10,000 in freight.

4. Before the beginning of its settlement by the Salvation Army there was but one house on all this land; now there must be quite sixty.

5. The history of the Colony is, in some respects, unfortunate. It was purchased in 1898 from the Amity Land and Irrigation Company for the sum of $47,000, or about £9,500. None of the purchase price was paid down, as the Salvation Army had not sufficient funds in hand at the time, and they still owe about $20,000, or £4,000, under this head.

5 *

6. The land having been bought, families were by degrees imported, for the most part from Chicago or other cities, and settled upon 20-acre lots. Hardly any of these settlers possessed capital; indeed, in many instances the Salvation Army was obliged to pay the cost of their transportation to their future homes. Moreover, few of them had experience in agriculture, although certain men with such experience were selected for their instruction in that art, and to this end placed among them as colonists.

7. At the present moment there are upon the Colony thirty-eight settlers, of whom six are "renters" or tenants. Since the inauguration of the venture, sixteen or eighteen families have left; some because they were not satisfied with the results; some because they found a rural life distasteful; some because of ill-health, and some because they thought that they could do better elsewhere. The Salvation Army, however, incurred no pecuniary loss through the departure of these colonists.

8. Of the remainder it may be said that, taking their class and resources into consideration, they have almost without exception prospered well, as will be seen by reference to the individual statements and accounts hereto annexed.

9. Had these men remained in their various situations in the cities it seems probable, if we may argue from what they achieved in the past, that, although they might have continued to make a living, they would not have put by any money. As it is, however, at the present moment, the total value of their equity (that is of all their possessions and interests over their liabilities to the Salvation Army and others) appears to be by the sworn accounts furnished me over $37,000, say, £7,400, or, roughly speaking, more than £200 per head. This cannot be considered as other than a very satisfactory result, if looked at from the point of view of the settlers. Indeed, this appears to be their own opinion.

10. When we turn, however, to the position of the Salvation Army, as regards the Amity Colony, the matter is different. In this case, reference to the accounts and to the statements of its officers, will show that it has made a net and unrecoverable loss of $23,111, or about £4,600. It should be noticed, however, that a great proportion of this

loss is due to the Army's somewhat rash attempt to carry on so extensive a venture without cash resources, and by means of capital borrowed at the high rate of interest of 5 or 6 per cent. Had the money been borrowed at, say, 3½ per cent., much of the loss would vanish.

11. Further, it would seem that the Salvation Army has made the error of not charging the colonists a sufficiently high price for the land, and of not taking into consideration many expenses connected with that land, which it has been unable to ask its settlers to reimburse. In short, it has bought its experience at a cost of under £5,000, which, when everything connected with the place, and the difficulties that it has been called upon to encounter, is considered, I do not, however, hold to be a great sum in view of the results achieved.

12. Broadly stated, these results may be said to include the turning of a block of waste prairie land into a prosperous settlement, where a population of about 275 persons are living in happiness, health, and comfort, with a good prospect of becoming entirely independent, and, in sundry instances, comparatively wealthy.

13. I will go further and add that when the circumstances are borne in mind, it seems to me remarkable that the loss, which has almost certainly reached its climax, has not been greater.

14. To begin with, for such land the price, which averaged about £5 per acre, was high, since it must be remembered that the soil was utterly unimproved, being mere naked prairie.

15. Also I am of opinion that, rich as it may be, it is not eminently suited to the purposes of colonisation, since much accurate levelling was required to get the water on to it, and the character of the sod, or turf, is very tough and hard to subdue. Indeed, it takes several years to make it really productive, although now almost every sort of crop and stock are raised upon it ; also apiculture is practised, and with it poultry rearing.

16. Further, although this was not foreseen at first, alkalis, or natural salts, have manifested themselves in many places, which alkali can only be got rid of by deep draining—sometimes with tiles—a very costly process in America. Then

the district is quite devoid of lumber, with the result that every fence, pole, or bit of timber for building must be bought at great expense.

17. Yet all these troubles have been, or are still in course of being surmounted, at a cost of a net loss to the originators of the enterprise of under £5,000, including interest payable on the money borrowed to enable them to carry it out. On the whole, therefore, these results cannot be thought un-satisfactory.

18. To turn to the more pleasing side of the picture, where seven years ago there was a waste may now be seen the homes and the population that I have already mentioned ; intelligent children, whose appearance shows health such as I have not noticed in American cities, being educated in well-built schools, and all the beginnings of a country town.

19. Thus, I inspected a post office, a blacksmith's shop, a grain store, a drug store, two meat markets or butchers, a drapery store, a hardware store, where everything is sold from agricultural implements down, a grocery store, kept by one of the pioneer colonists, a local bank, known as the Bank of Amity, which was started with a capital of $5,000, put up by the colonists and others, and is doing well, a " Mail-order " house, where everything may be obtained at the price marked in a printed catalogue, which is stocked with £1,200 worth of goods, a newspaper office, a barber's shop, and so forth.

20. In another place is a large sanatorium, capable of accommodating forty or fifty patients, that is to be used for consumptives, who benefit greatly by this healthy air, though whether it is wise to introduce sufferers from tuberculosis into an agricultural settlement is a question which I will not argue.

21. Further, the land which produced nothing but buffalo grass, now rears cattle, horses, and sheep, and bears many kinds of crops, including Kaffir corn, fruits and vegetables, the famous canteloupe melons, and, notably, sugar-beet, that, owing to the presence of a factory which is in course of erection in the neighbourhood, is becoming the safest and most renumerative crop in the district.

Such, in brief, are the results of the establishment of the Amity Colony.

22. I submit that the lesson to be learned from it is one of great importance. It shows that unskilled and untrained persons can be taken from towns, put upon land and thrive there, even when that land is of a nature not very suitable to such settlements. That this should have been demonstrated at the cost of a loss of £5,000 incurred purely through mistakes and inexperience is, in my opinion, a great and remarkable gain.

23. In concluding these Remarks I wish to allude to the spirit of mutual friendliness which evidently animates the colonists of Fort Amity.

24. Never have I seen such a spirit more clearly and happily demonstrated than I did at a village feast, or banquet, which was given in my honour in the principal schoolhouse of the Colony. At this festivity were gathered some 250 people, in fact, every person who could possibly attend. Some of these made speeches; among them a woman, who was one of the first comers, and an ex-constable of the London Metropolitan Police, who is now a colonist here, and has recently been elected to the important post of Sheriff of the County.

25. All these speeches were dominated by two notes: that of the complete contentment of the speakers with their lot, and that of their affectionate regard for their fellow colonists, and for the Salvation Army, which had enabled them to attain to their present positions. That these sentiments were by no means individual to the speakers was clear also from the loud and hearty cheers wherewith they were greeted by the audience.

26. At this feast an address of welcome was presented to my daughter and myself by some of the leading colonists, on behalf of the entire community, and when read was received with much applause, thus showing that it expressed the views of all present. I will quote a short passage from it, since it demonstrates that the colonists are not afraid of formally setting down their opinions as to the benefits which they have received, and that others are likely to receive to whom similar advantages are offered, from such a scheme of land settlement as is in force at Fort Amity.

" We hope that what you have seen with your own eyes and what you have heard from our lips, also the figures which we have given you of our standing and condition before coming here, and our standing of to-day with your own influence and your own personality, will have such effect in interesting capital in similar enterprises as will result in an almost universal application of this plan.

"We would like the benefits which we—our families and children—are receiving to be extended to the thousands who have been longing and praying for such a chance."

27. I do not know that I can end my Remarks better than with these words, which clearly demonstrate how the whole matter is regarded by those chiefly interested in it, namely, folk, who, having been taken from a life of hard and prospectless labour in the cities, are now happy and well-to-do householders and owners of land.

H. RIDER HAGGARD,
Commissioner.

No. 20.

FORT AMITY COLONY.

NOTES OF AN INTERVIEW BETWEEN COMMISSIONER H. RIDER HAGGARD AND VARIOUS OFFICERS OF THE SALVATION ARMY.

5TH APRIL, 1905.

Before starting to inspect the Colony the following conversation took place. The names of the persons present are as follows, *viz.* : Commander Booth Tucker, Commissioner Kilbey, Colonel Holland, Staff-Captain Hamon, Staff-Captain Durand, Miss Angela R. Haggard, and Mr. Harry Wright.

The interview was opened by the Commissioner, who asked Commander Booth Tucker the following question :—

Q. Will you please tell me the history of this Colony ? Set out what you all honestly believe to be its present condition and its future prospects.

A. Commander Booth Tucker : This Colony was founded in 1898. It will be the seventh anniversary on the 18th of this month (April). The choice of the land was preceded by a good deal of preliminary inquiry. The plan to "put the waste labour on the waste land by means of the waste capital and thus convert this trinity of waste into a unity of production" seemed to strike home to the people as a possible and feasible one. This alludes to the American public in general. As a result we were invited by the Santa Fé Railroad Company to inspect lands for settlement along their lines. We travelled from Chicago as far as Arizona, inspecting different tracts of land, and the Railway Company highly recommended this particular tract to us. We knew they had means of information which were not at our disposal, and that we could thoroughly rely upon the President, Mr. Ripley, and some of the other officials, who were personal friends of the Army, to watch our interests and see that we had a good selection of land. We also had experts from Rocky Ford, Colorado, to test the land, etc. Even after we had the recommendation of the Railway, we had the land inspected by agricultural experts. In addition, a tract of 70,000 acres was owned by the Amity Land and Irrigation Company, a powerful and reputable Company, with its headquarters in New York, who were prepared to offer us easy terms of payment, and as I was a great believer in irrigation, from my knowledge of it in India, and wanted to see a Colony formed on an irrigated tract of land, and this particular Company had already put in their irrigation works, so that the land was, in a sense, ready, everything was there.

Q. I understand it was bare and unimproved prairie?

A. Commander Booth Tucker: Yes; we had the chance of choosing between the upland and what is now the Colony land. The point that influenced us in the preference of this land was the abundance of the water supply. First we had a good ditch with an abundant flow, which had never been known to fail. Second, we had an underflow about ten feet from the surface, which was available for cattle and ordinary household purposes; not good for drinking, but good for other purposes, and which was also limitless. Further, we had an artesian supply of pure water, at a depth of from 200 to 400 feet.

Q. Therefore you had three separate supplies?

A. Commander Booth Tucker: Yes; our water supply was absolutely safe. So we bought this land. We bought it on time payments; one section of 640 acres, which we increased afterwards to 1,760 acres.

Q. What price did you pay?

A. Commander Booth Tucker: The first cash purchase price was $20 (say, £4) per acre, and the last was $27.50 (say, £5 10s.) per acre.

Q. What have you done in the way of paying off that purchase price?

A. Commander Booth Tucker: The first portion we have paid for entirely. The total price amounted to $47,000 (say, £9,500). We still owe about $20,000 (say, £4,000).

Q. Are you keeping up the payments?

A. Commander Booth Tucker: Yes; we are paying our instalments regularly. They amount to a little over $3,000 annually.

Q. When do you expect to make your last payment?

A. Commander Booth Tucker: The last payment will be made within six or seven years.

Q. What steps did you take towards settling?

A. Commander Booth Tucker: Most of the first batch of fourteen families were selected in Chicago. It was a time of great financial distress in that city. We selected a number of good, desirable families.

Q. What do you mean, Commander Booth Tucker, by good, desirable families?

A. Commander Booth Tucker: They were all family men, with two exceptions, with nice families, really worthy of assistance, and they have answered our expectations.

Q. Were they in narrow circumstances when you selected them?

A. Colonel Holland: We had to pay the transportation expenses of every family, save one, and in some instances even to pay for food which they consumed on the journey. But they were all worthy poor.

Q. Were they of the same class as we find in our cities in England?

A. Commander Booth Tucker: Yes; of the same class as there are in our English cities.

Q. Were these people agriculturists, or in any way connected with the land, or typical city dwellers?

A. Colonel Holland: They were all taken from the city. With the exception of about five heads of families, they had either been on farms or worked on farms in the past. But at the time they were taken they were city dwellers, and had been so for some time. As regards the other heads of families, they had no agricultural experience.

I should add that there are now thirty-eight farmers, including six renters or tenants.

Q. Well, as regards the balance, what were they?

A. Colonel Holland: Several of these latter importations were labourers, representing almost all classes of city labour, such as street car conductors, warehousemen, waggon drivers, and two or three were town carpenters.

Q. Then I take it, gentlemen, that practically this Colony is formed of folk from the city?

A. Colonel Holland: Almost entirely, with the exception

of a few experienced men who were sandwiched in as
" pace-setters " and " examples ".

Q. Where did those examples come from ?

A. Colonel Holland : Two or three were picked up in this
particular district; the others from various States in the
Middle-West.

Q. Will you kindly tell me, Colonel Holland, what
happened after you got your population on the land ?

A. Colonel Holland : I had better begin my answer to
your question by saying that we made a mistake in not
having the land broken up and under process of cultivation
before we placed these inexperienced persons on it, for the
reason that, as Commander Booth Tucker has explained, we
located on bottom land, covered by a heavy native sod,
which took almost three years to pulverise and sweeten.
The first year was, in consequence, devoted to breaking up
land, building houses, and constructing irrigation ditches,
instead of engaging in the actual work of raising crops.

Q. How were your people maintained during this period
of preparation ?

A. Colonel Holland : Not having land capable of profitable cultivation, and having to engage in the work I have
described, consisting of land-breaking, building, ditch-making,
etc., it was necessary for us to maintain the families during
this period by means of cash loans, to be repaid, which
loans averaged in amount to from $2 to $4 per family per
week, and were, you will understand, charged against them.

By the beginning of the second season our land, while not
in a good condition for the growing of crops, had been so
worked upon by our colonists as to be in fair tilth and condition, and reasonable crops were obtained that year as a
result.   During this period more colonists were imported.
By this time we found it possible to discontinue the maintenance loans, already referred to, and until they realised upon
their next crop, our people were able to maintain themselves
by such labour as they could procure off their farms, either
for the Army or for others who were willing to pay them.
But all work done by the colonists on his own holding and
for his own benefit was unremunerated, nor were any further
loans made to such parties, except under circumstances so
special that I need not enter into them.

Q. That about covers the situation. Now I want you to tell me what have been the results. How are these colonists doing?

A. Colonel Holland: From the period referred to until the present time, our settlers have been, generally speaking, self-supporting. That is to say, they have been able to maintain their families without the aid of loans, and have, moreover, during this time, added considerably to their own holdings, in the shape of buildings and other improvements and in the accumulation of stock, some of which, as you will see from their individual statements, is considerable. They met with a difficulty, however, in the matter of alkali, which began to appear in certain parts after the land had been put under thorough cultivation, which difficulty, however, is still being dealt with by means of drainage, and will, we believe, be entirely mastered.

Q. Are the colonists then now in a prosperous condition generally? Have any of them failed and departed? If so, how many?

A. Colonel Holland: As I have pointed out, prosperity has been very much retarded owing to the causes given, but, as already stated, our people are self-supporting. They are making some payments on their places, improving their buildings, dealing with this excessive moisture and alkali condition, and are very confident that each year will see them in a more prosperous state. They are certainly in a more flourishing condition than ever they would have been had they remained in the city, where they would have been the recipients of a living wage only, provided they could still continue to earn it. Here they have not only lived—better probably than they would have lived in the city—but most of them have acquired substantial proprietary interests in their holdings, which are destined to increase from year to year. I think I can say, therefore, that they are in a comparatively prosperous condition.

With reference to the second head of your question, I would say, yes; some of them failed. That is to say they have not been satisfied with the results they were obtaining, and sixteen or eighteen families have moved away. Of course, there have been various causes leading up to this, but since they are not now on the ground, I suppose you would consider them as failures. It should be understood, however, that they have not all departed because they could not get a living out of the land. Two or three of them left because of ill-health, either on the part of the men or members of their family, and some of them thought they could do better elsewhere as farmers. Let me illustrate :—

A number of our colonists were Canadians by birth, and with the opening up of free land in the Canadian North-West, several of our families moved away there. In one or two other cases, men who were mechanics took up small agricultural holdings near large towns, in which they supposed they could get some employment at their trades.

Q. Did those persons who left the Colony satisfy their indebtedness to you before they departed ?

A. Colonel Holland : In almost every case they did, either by payment or by improvements, which they transferred to us at an appraised value, or by the sale of their holdings to other persons. In fact, in a number of instances our settlers moved away with considerable money as a result of their occupation of holdings here. I may add that we found no difficulty in filling the places of those who departed by other settlers. In fact, the departing colonist himself usually succeeded without trouble in finding a purchaser for what rights he had in his holding. I may also add that instead of finding it difficult to get colonists to occupy each vacant allotment, we are simply inundated with applications from the most desirable of people, who plead with us to give them a chance to acquire a home in the country.

Staff-Captain Durand (Manager of Fort Amity Colony) : At the present moment every acre of land fit for cultivation is occupied by the colonists, or renters, for I should explain to you our system is to sell 20 acres to the individual and to allow him to rent another 20.

I should like to say here that our principal reason for renting out a portion of the land is, that it may be gotten into suitable condition to sell to a permanent settler.

Colonel Holland : I should like to explain that here our conditions are peculiar, for, as Commander Booth Tucker pointed out, that in order to obtain the benefits of a sure water supply, we located on bottom land, which very much retarded our progress at the start and has been the cause of the alkali conditions already referred to. In future experiments of this nature we should be careful to select land that would drain itself naturally and whose sod would lend itself to subjugation the first year.

Speaking generally, I may say that as a purely land-selling proposition, our whole transaction in connection with this Colony would produce a handsome margin over all liabilities, that is including interest, taxes and water assessments. In fact, there has been such an appreciation in the value of our holdings by reason of the improvements thereon and the general settlement of the district, that most of the land which we and the colonists possess would sell for twice what we paid for it.

Q. Now, Commander, I want you and Colonel Holland to tell me if you are satisfied on the whole with your experiment, and whether you consider that this experiment could be applied on a large scale, and, if so, under what conditions?

A. Commander Booth Tucker: I am more than ever satisfied as to the soundness of the general principles, and am certain that they can be applied to any extent should the necessary capital be available. I consider it to be a sound business proposition.

Q. As a sound business proposition?

A. Commander Booth Tucker: Yes; as a sound business proposition. We have learned by the mistakes we have made to avoid them in the future. For instance, we have found that it was absolutely necessary to have a sufficiency of capital at the outset and not to depend upon raising it as we went along.

Q. Is the Salvation Army sufficiently satisfied with these experiments to be willing, in the event of the provision of such capital, to undertake its application in the direction of selecting suitable persons to place upon the land and to undertake the management of such settlements on a large scale?

A. Commander Booth Tucker: I think we could now safely do it. The experience of this last seven years has furnished us with the qualified managers for such an undertaking, which is, perhaps, one of the most necessary conditions of success.

Q. You say you could safely do it. Would you, or rather the Salvation Army, be prepared to do it?

A. Commander Booth Tucker: Yes; to any extent. Land is abundant throughout the world. The people of the cities are hungering for the opportunity of getting at it. They only want leadership and business management. The only requisite that I see that is absolutely not to be gotten over is a supply of the necessary capital. Our experience goes to show that the man without money makes a better average colonist and a better average settler than the man with money, and it seems to me a radical mistake that this and other countries should confine their settlements to the man with money, and ignore the man whose capital consists of brain and muscle, but who can be turned into a prosperous " home owner ". I suppose, Mr. Commissioner, that the average " equity " of the settlers on this Colony, after paying all that is due from them, lies between $500 and $3,000. Of course, some have much more than others, as a result of their superior intelligence, powers of work or good fortune. For instance, a man I was talking to on this Colony yesterday said to me : " I suppose I am worth $5,000. Now it is calculated that the most a working man can lay aside in the city is about $100 per year, and not more than one in thirty can do that. Whereas, after seven years on this Colony, I have earned $5,000, not all of it, it is true, out of the land, but out of ventures connected with my holdings on the land. I had not a dollar when I came here."

Colonel Holland: Further answering your question, Mr. Commissioner, as to the practicability of our plan for the settlement of poor people on the land, I would like to say that I don't think the degree of success that we have met with at Amity should be taken as any criterion of what would be possible under such conditions as I know are available in different parts of the world. It is my emphatic opinion that the industry and intelligence manifested by our settlers here has been such as would have produced triumphant success in nine out of every ten Colonies undertaken under more favourable conditions.

(As the figures and information necessary to satisfy the Commissioner were not forthcoming at the time, and had to be got out, the inquiry was here adjourned till the next day, when the same persons were present, and the following questions were put, and the answers to them given.)

Q. What do you consider to be the present financial condition of the Colony?

A. Staff-Captain Hamon: The present financial position of the Colony, as regards the Salvation Army, shows a net loss of $23,111.50 (or about £4,600), which loss must be written off. It should be observed, however, that the said loss includes interest to the amount of $25,162, paid by the Salvation Army on loans contracted at the rate of 5 and 6 per cent., as the Salvation Army began to run this Colony without any cash capital.

Q. Are you solvent?

A. Staff-Captain Hamon: As regards the matter of our solvency, taking this Colony individually, the Army has lost the sum which I have quoted; in short, it has paid between £4,000 and £5,000 for its experience, spread over seven years, and including every sort of charge, foreseen and unforeseen. With that experience thus obtained, such loss would be scarcely likely to recur in any subsequent experiment, especially as we have had to meet many unforeseen conditions, such as alkali, and also certain seasons of great difficulty, including heavy hail storms, a total crop failure in one season and a flood in another.

Q. In the event of a sale, would there be back in your pockets everything you have spent?

A. Commander Booth Tucker: As regards your question, in the event of a sale, supposing the colonists' proportion to be deducted and only the equity of the Salvation Army to be sold, we should lose the above stated amount, that is between £4,000 and £5,000; but if our equity in the colonists' property should be included, we should then stand to have a surplus of assets over liabilities to the amount of $15,026.99, or, roughly speaking, £3,000. In this is not included any increased valuation for the town site, where land has been selling at the rate of from $600 to $3,000 per acre.

Q. Would the colonists receive all they have spent?

A. Staff-Captain Durand: Yes; and in addition $37,943.77 (say, £7,588).

6

Q. Would there be anything over, either in your pocket or in that of the colonists?

A. Staff-Captain Hamon: I have already answered this question. There would be a loss to us of between £4,000 and £5,000, and a gain to the colonists of $37,943.77 (or £7,588).

Q. Now what did you really pay for the land?

A. Staff-Captain Hamon: We paid for the land $47,000 (or £9,400).

Q. What are its present values and what are those of the improvements thereon?

A. Staff-Captain Hamon: The present values, with improvements thereon, as per sworn appraisement, amount to $154,775. The Sanatorium building is not included in these figures, either as regards prime cost or as regards present values, except as regards the site.

Q. What would the settlement fetch as a " going " concern?

A. Staff-Captain Hamon: I cannot answer that question. We can only rely upon the appraiser's valuations, which, however, to the best of our knowledge and experience we believe to be quite correct, and, indeed, very conservative.

Q. Have you obtained outside valuations?

A. Staff-Captain Hamon: Yes; we hand you herewith the valuations, attested by a reliable appraiser, who, I believe, has given a very conservative estimate.

Q. The Commissioner to Commander Booth Tucker: Does not the fact that you have lost £4,000 while the colonists are already between £7,000 and £8,000 in pocket over and above their liabilities, suggest to you that you must have sold the land to those colonists at too low a figure, and without making sufficient allowance for further expenses which you would be called upon to incur in connection with such land?

A. Commander Booth Tucker: I think that it not only suggests this, it proves it. This was one of our errors of judgment for which we must pay. It is not likely to occur again.

H. RIDER HAGGARD,
Commissioner.

F. BOOTH TUCKER.
JAMES H. DURAND.
ALFRED HAMON.
THOMAS HOLLAND.

A GROUP OF COLONISTS, FORT AMITY.

COLONISTS HARVESTING KAFIR CORN.

No. 21.

INTERVIEWS WITH COLONISTS AT FORT AMITY COLONY,

5th, 6th, 7th APRIL, 1905.

L. A. DOBLE :—

Valuation . . .	$2,925.00 (or about) £585	
Amount owing Salvation Army and others	2,038.72	„ 407
Equity . .	$886.28	„ £178

I have been here three years. Came from Sioux City, Nebraska. I was a tinsmith. All I had was $10 when I arrived. I took a 20-acre lot. I have made a living and more since I came here. The land was rough, and I had buildings to put up. The Army advanced me the money to do this. I have not been able to pay the Army anything off land or money advanced. I have been putting all money made into improvements and stock. I would not like to sell my place, and would not care to put a price upon it. My equity shows $997.28, but I should not like to take twice that amount. I have been raising sugar beets, but, principally, dairying. I sell the sugar beets to the factory. I am glad I came here. Am better satisfied than I have been in any other place. Have been a great deal in this and other countries, and find great advantages here. The Army's arrangements have been of great benefit and assistance to me. I could never have done what I have without that organisation. I expect to commence paying the Army for loans as soon as I get my dairy put in proper shape. I have forty-eight head of cattle.

NOTE.—Mr. Doble seems a very well-educated and intelligent man.—H. R. H.

W. J. GRINDROD :—

Valuation . . .	$2,660.00 (or about) £532	
Amount owing Salvation Army and others	2,357.00	„ 471
Equity . .	$303.00	„ £61

6 *

I came from St. Joseph, Missouri, one year ago. Am
married, with seven children. I was working in a packing
house. Had no capital when I came to Amity. I only
just earned a living when I was working in St. Joseph, and
thought I should like to try something else. Have been
stock raising since I married. I have fifteen milk cows,
seven yearlings, eight spring calves, six horses, nine hogs,
forty chickens. I am farming 108 acres—20 bought and
88 rented. I am going to put 20 acres in beets this
year. Am satisfied with the outlook. Am glad I came out
of the city, and shall soon be able to pay off what I am
owing.

O. M. PRINGLE :—

Valuation . . .	$2,475.00 (or about)	£495
Amount owing Salvation Army and others	1,185.88 ,,	237
Equity. .	$1,289.12 ,,	£258

I have been here three years, but have only had two
seasons on farm. Am married and have three children. I
came from Hennessey, Oklahoma Territory. I was a land
agent in that town. I had a capital of $1,700. I only owe
money on land to Army. I put up my own buildings and
own my own stock. I am a gardener and fruit raiser, and
was put on this Colony to instruct others. Have made a
living on the place. Am glad I came, and I look forward
to making a success on the place. I have four horses, four
milk cows, and six calves. At present I am making a living
by sale of cream and eggs. My land is not in order yet. I am
farming about 50 acres, 20 of which I have bought, and 30 I
am renting from the Army. I rent on the share crop system.

S. INMAN :—

Valuation . . .	$2,522.00 (or about)	£504
Amount owing Salvation Army and others	1,954.10 ,,	390
Equity . .	$567.90 ,,	£114

Have been here about four years. Am married and have
a wife and five children. I am from North-East Kansas.

Was farming before I came to Amity. Had no capital when
I arrived here, but had a little stock. Have been making a
living since I came here, but have not been able to pay much
off my land. I am not sorry I came. I like the climate. I
reckon my prospects fully as good as they were in Kansas.

GEORGE NICOL :—
Valuation . . .	$2,498.00 (or about)	£499
Amount owing Salvation Army and others	1,841.40 ,,	368
Equity . .	**$656.60** ,,	**£131**

I have been here nearly five years. Am married and have
four children. Was a carpenter in Chicago before coming
here. I only had $25 when I came. Have not done a
great deal in farming since I came ; have been building my
house, which is a very nice one, and getting my stock, etc.
Have not paid any cash on account of money owing the
Army, but have done a great deal of work which has been
credited to me. Prospects are very good now, and we
expect to do well in the future.

I am putting in 25 acres of beets this year, and three
acres of canteloupes. Am very glad I came here. I think
I should have made a mistake had I not done so. I came
from Glasgow to this country.

D. COKER :—
Valuation . . .	$3,540.00 (or about)	£708
Amount owing Salvation Army and others	1,326.67 ,,	265
Equity . .	**$2,213.33** ,,	**£443**

I have been here seven years. Am a married man with
seven children. I came from Chicago and was a painter.
I came here to try and get a home of my own. I had $13
capital when I arrived. I have done pretty fairly here.
Have made some payments to the Army. Am very glad I
came, and am looking forward to doing well. I run a little
restaurant and boarding house as well as my farm. We
have been injured a great deal through alkali on our land.

Have four head of cattle and two horses. Notwithstanding a run of hard luck have done very well, and am glad I came here.

NOTE.—This man had no knowledge whatever of agriculture or farming when he came here.—H. R. H.

CHARLES BARKMAN :—

Valuation . . .	$2,435.00 (or about)	£487
Amount owing Salvation Army and others	1,914.41 ,,	382
Equity . .	$520.59 ,,	£105

I have been here six years. Came from Kansas City, where I was engaged in butter and cheese selling. I had no capital when I arrived. The reason I came was because I wanted to get out of the city. I am a married man with five children. I have done as well as I could expect here, having been unfortunate in getting allotted to me the worst land on the Colony. The land has been greatly improved through draining. I think I am all right now. My farm did well last year, and I am well satisfied. I have thirty-two head of cattle and six head of horses. I have not paid much to the Army, but I figure my increased stock meets it all. Had my land been drained the same as it is now, I could have made all my payments. I am very glad, indeed, I came here. I had a rather discouraging time when I first came here, owing to my farm not being properly drained, but now it is all right, and I figure I have got a good promising place. I go in for raising cattle, which, I think, pays better than dairying.

J. A. ZIEGLER :—

Valuation . . .	$3,405.00 (or about)	£681
Amount owing Salvation Army and others	2,182.00 ,,	436
Equity . .	$1,223.00 ,,	£245

I have been here three years. Am married and have three children. Came from Sioux City, Iowa. Had charge of a section in a grocery store. Had been there ten years. I came here to visit my father; liked the place; found the climate was good for me; and stayed on. Had $125 before buying my ticket here. Am well satisfied with the Colony. Have forty-five head of cattle and ten horses. Have paid small amount to the Army off stock. Have been holding my cattle as last year they were bringing bad prices; shall do better this year. Have got a good crop of wheat, and everything looks very promising. Am very glad I came here. Have got a good bunch of cows and doing very well. Would not like a position as grocery clerk again on any account, as prospects, I consider, are very bright here.

NOTE.—This man, it will be seen, has been ten years in a grocery store, and had saved $125. He has been two years on the Colony, and his equity is valued at $1,222.46. —H. R. H.

ERIK ERICKSON :—

Valuation	.	.	$2,495.00	(or about) £499	
Amount owing Salvation Army and others			1,911.78	,,	382
Equity	.	.	$583.22	,,	£117

I have been here seven years, am married, and have two children. Have done quite as well as I could expect. Brought $25 capital. Was a street car conductor in Chicago before coming to Amity. I came here because I could see no future before me. My specialities have been beets, alfalfa and stock. Have twenty head of cattle and four horses. Am farming 80 acres, 20 purchased and 60 rented, payments being made in kind, one-seventh of sugar beet crop and one-half alfalfa. I reckon I am $682 ahead of all my liabilities; meanwhile I have lived well and enjoyed good health. Am glad I undertook this venture. I look forward to paying all I owe, and making a success of life. I reckon this Colony Scheme is the only one possible for men like me. It gave me an opportunity to start and I am thankful for it.

JOHN DAVEY :—

Valuation . . .	$2,985.00 (or about)	£597
Amount owing Salvation Army and others	904.28	,,	181
Equity . .	$2,080.72	,,	£416

I have been at Amity for four years as a colonist. Was
a Salvation Army Officer for three years before that. I am
married and have one child. Had no capital. I have been
doing very well. My specialities have been beets and alfalfa.
Have paid Army $500 off the amount I borrowed. Have
had an offer of $2,000 for my place alone, without stock. I
owe the Army $900. I am well satisfied with my position
here, and shall soon be able to pay the Army off what I owe.

WILLIAM SACHTLER :—

Valuation . . .	$2,270.00 (or about)	£454
Amount owing Salvation Army and others	2,285.91	,,	457
Minus . .	$15.91	,,	£3

I have been on the Colony two years. Was an iron
moulder before I came here from South Norwalk, Connecticut. Had $25 when I came here. Have wife and six
children. I came here through offer of the Salvation Army.
Have been doing pretty well. Have not paid Army anything in cash, but have done considerable work, which has
been credited to my account. Have built a nice house of
stone, which I would not sell for $1,100. I borrowed $350
from Army to build it. Am quite satisfied with the Colony
and glad I came. My specialities are beets and canteloupes.
I think the outlook bright.

J. H. NEWMAN :—

Valuation. . .	$7,530.00 (or about)	£1,506
Amount owing Salvation Army and others . . .	2,223.00	,,	444
Equity .	$5,307.00	,,	£1,062

I have been here seven years, am married and have four children. I was a carpenter in Chicago before coming to Amity. I had no capital, none whatever, although I received $50 for work done in Chicago some time after I came to Amity. I have done very well here. It is claimed that a labouring man in the States cannot put away under the best circumstances more than $100 per year. I have cleared in seven years $4,000 at least, so I think I have done very well indeed. I have paid a good deal of my indebtedness back to the Army. I am a little behind owing to a failure of crops two years ago, which made it impossible for farmers to pay me accounts in connection with a little hardware business I run as well as my farm. I am very glad I came here. I think it is a grand opening for a poor man.

NOTE.—Mr. Newman is a highly respectable and intelligent man; indeed I should say a person of ability. —H. R. H.

ROBERT FREWING :—

Valuation	.	.	$2,615.00	(or about)	£523
Amount owing Salvation Army and others			1,618,00	,,	323
Equity	.		$997.00	,,	£200

(Robert Frewing being absent, his son was interviewed.)

I am the son of Robert Frewing—twenty-three years old. I came here with my father seven years ago. He was a plasterer in Chicago. There were seven of us—five children —with mother and father. Father has done very nicely here. We have not paid much back to the Army in cash, but have considerable credits for work done for the organisation. We value our place at $2,500, and owe the Army $1,600. We are going to raise ten acres of beets this year. I personally have ten head of cattle. I farm with my father. Am very happy here, and so are father and mother. It is nicer than living in Chicago. I like it better.

NOTE.—A very bright and intelligent young man with a pleasant face and frank eyes.—H. R. H.

CHAS. B. GAYLORD :—

Valuation . . .	$2,220.00	(or about) £444	
Amount owing Salvation Army and others	1,555.00	,,	311 .
Equity .	$665.00	,,	£133

I came here from Chicago, where I was engaged as a car conductor. I had no capital. Had worked for years in the city, but had saved nothing. I have a wife and three children, and my brother also lives with me. I came here as I was anxious to try to secure a home of my own, and besides, I wanted to start the bee industry, of which I had had some knowledge as an amateur. I find it pleasant here, and the prospects very bright. I intend making a speciality of bee culture, but shall do farming as well. Am putting in 10 acres of beet, the rest in other crops, but beets and bees will be the principal things I shall give my attention to. I am sure I shall be able to pay the Army all I owe in half the time allowed, namely, six years.

I have had a short experience here, and am more than satisfied with my venture. I hope to bring my family up here and become a permanent settler. I want nothing better than this; I am well satisfied with my lot, and am very happy. My wife found it trying at first, being so far from her friends, but is now quite contented, and as happy as I am.

NOTE.—This man seems particularly happy and a bright and intelligent fellow. He has had a very good education, and in his early days had three years' experience in a medical college. He had not the finances to go through.—H. R. H.

G. PRIEBE :—

Valuation . . .	$2,295.00	(or about) £459	
Amount owing Salvation Army and others	2,477.00	,,	495
Minus .	$182.00	,,	£36

I have been here four and a half years. Came from Ohio, where I was a Salvation Army Officer. Previous to that I was working in a garden, at general gardening work. I had only $3 when I came here with my wife and three children. I have not done very well as I had a serious set-back with the alkali. With the draining that we are doing on the Colony things are sure to be improved greatly, I fancy. I have no equity in my land, etc., after meeting my liabilities. If I had not been unfortunate with the alkali I should have done very well. I am afraid I cannot pay the Army in the twelve-year limit, but believe I can in twenty years.

The prospects are better and the future looks brighter for everybody here.

I have two milk cows, three yearlings, and seven heifer calves, one horse and four colts.

GEORGE WAIDNER :—

Valuation . . . $2,080.00 (or about)	£416
Amount owing Salvation Army and others 2,353.00 ,,	470
Minus . . $273.00 ,,	£54

I came here four years ago from Baltimore, Maryland, where I was working as a packer in a provision house. I had no capital; had to borrow the money from the Army to come. I have one child and my mother-in-law lives with me. I have paid the Army a little of my indebtedness, but not as much as I should. I expect to do much better in the future, as I am getting my land into better condition. It has been a rather hard proposition. I am putting in 8 acres of beets, 2 acres of canteloupes, and 10 acres in feed.

I have three cows, three horses and two calves. I am glad I came to Amity, as I find the climate so much better for my wife, who was almost an invalid before I came. She is now quite strong and well.

The prospects here are better than ever they have been. We have learned a great deal. Did not know a thing about cows or farming of any description; we can now manage very well as we understand the work. I guess my holdings are worth more than the amount I owe the Army, but I should not like to say how much.

THOS. CLOUGHLEY:—

Valuation . . .	$2.315.00 (or about)	£463
Amount owing Salvation Army and others	1,618.00 ,,	323
Equity .	$697.00 ,,	£140

I have been here two months. Came from the City of Omaha, Nebraska, where I was working as an engineer. I had $17.50 per week there, and managed by careful living to save about $800. I, therefore, had this capital when I came to the Colony. I came here first on account of my wife's health, and second, because ever since it opened I have been anxious for a home on the Colony. I consider it a better place than a city for bringing up children, of which I have five. I believe I shall do well here, though I know I shall have to work. I have put in 9 acres of spring wheat, and my intentions are to put in 15 acres of beets and about 3 acres of oats. I have 20 acres that I bought from the Army, and 9 acres which I rent. I am glad I came here, for I believe the prospects for a man with energy and willing to work are of the best. I have four head of cattle and two horses.

JOSEPH HUGH HARGREAVES :—

Valuation . . .	$3,185.00 (or about)	£637
Amount owing Salvation Army and others	1,831.00 ,,	366
Equity . .	$1,354.00 ,,	£271

I was an officer in active service in the Salvation Army for twenty-one years before I came to the Colony. The reason of my coming here was principally because of my health. I was broken down, and, in fact, was given up by both friends and doctors. The Army suggested this place as a last resource, and I came unwillingly because I felt nothing could save me, and I would rather have remained with my friends. However, I am glad I came, for ever since the day

I landed I have felt benefited, and although I know I still have the weakness in my lungs, I am yet well, and able to do pretty nearly any work my farm calls for me to do. I believe I shall live here to be a good old age.

I had no capital when I came here. The Army advanced me the car fare; in fact, everything. I owe the Army about $1,800, and I reckon my house, stock, etc., worth at least $3,000, and I would not want to part with it for that. I am making chickens my speciality; I have 150, all of which are doing well. I have 20 acres which I bought from the Army, all in alfalfa and 20 rented (for part of produce), which is in beets and canteloupe. I have one of the prettiest houses on the Colony, and I am very proud of my house. I believe the future has a great share of brightness and prosperity in store for Amity.

NOTE.—I visited Mr. Hargreaves' house, which is a really excellent dwelling, and built of stone.—H. R. H.

C. STIMSON :—

All obligations paid off; value of property has not been furnished.

I have been here six years. Came from West Kansas. I was farming there, and brought with me about $1,000. I paid for my land to the Army, all cash, which cost $600. I put up my stone cottage myself. I consider I have done very well here, and am glad I came. There are many advantages over the place I left. There was no one living within three miles of me, whilst here I have the advantage of being on the Colony with all the company I want. I have four children, and it is a great advantage having them near a school. I do general farming, stock, beets, alfalfa, bees, chickens, etc. I am making a good living and consider I am doing fairly well, and reckon I am getting ahead every year. I have a nice cottage built with stone; barn and chicken house are also built with stone and very solid.

W. L. STEVENS :—

Valuation . . . $2,540.00 (or about)		£508
Amount owing Salvation Army and others 764.00	,,	153
Equity . . $1,776.00	,,	£355

I was an officer in the Salvation Army, and came here seven years ago on account of kidney trouble. I had about $150 capital when I landed at Amity with my wife and two children. I have done very well financially. I owe the Army now only $400, whilst my farm, etc., are worth $2,000. I have, therefore, an interest in the place of $1,600. I am well satisfied with this, for considering the little or no experience I had had of irrigated land I think I have done well. I have my 20 acres in alfalfa and wheat. Three years ago I left my farm here and returned to the Salvation Army work again, renting my place. I came back six weeks ago as I found my health was failing me again. I am better since I came back. I consider the prospects here very good, and the next two years will make a big difference in the place. The beet business will help considerably, and the land has been greatly improved recently by draining.

T. F. McABEE :—

Valuation . . .	$3,200.00 (or about)	£640
Amount owing Salvation Army and others	1,747.00 ,,	349
Equity . .	$1,453.00 ,,	£291

I have been here seven years. I came from Alliance, Ohio, where I was working in a grocery store. I am a married man, had one child when I came, but now have three. I had no capital when I came here ; it took me all my time to meet expenses and keep out of debt. I came here to better myself, being anxious to get a home of my own. I have done really well since coming to Amity, and am glad I ever got the chance of taking a place on the Colony. I am thankful to the Salvation Army for the opportunity. I calculate my house, land and stock is worth $3,000, while I owe the Army about $1,700. I have six head of cattle, two horses, and one yearling. This year I am putting in 15 acres of beets, and believe I am going to do very well.

NOTE.—Mr. McAbee is an intelligent man who seems much pleased with his place, and apparently has a very happy home. His wife is a superior woman.

The appraiser in going over this colonist's property omitted
to reckon the stone quarry, which is valued at $2,000, which
amount is not included in the statement showing the
financial position of the Amity colonists.

H. W. Manning :—

Valuation . . .	$3,281.00 (or about)	£656
Amount owing Salvation Army and others	1,834.00 ,,	367
Equity . .	$1,477.00 ,,	£289

I have been on the Colony eighteen months. I came
from Alamosa, Colorado, where I was farming. I did not
do very well, and having much sickness came here with my
wife and ten children. I had no capital, and could not have
come here were it not for the Army. I have done well in
Amity. I consider my place worth $2,500, including stock,
etc. I owe the Army $1,500, so have an equity of $1,000
in less than two years. My specialities are beets and alfalfa.
Have twelve head of cattle, four mules and three horses. I
appreciate most assuredly the comradeship we have on the
Colony. The prospects for the future are better than they
have ever been. We have a happy, prosperous time before
us.

Elmer E. Harris :—

Valuation . . .	$2,635.00 (or about)	£527
Amount owing Salvation Army and others	1,080.00 ,,	216
Equity . .	$1,555.00 ,,	£311

I came here six years ago from Cotton Wood Falls, Kansas,
where I was engaged in farming, working on my father's
place. I left Cotton Wood Falls with my team intending
to do freighting, etc., in the mountains. In passing through
Amity I met some one with whom I was acquainted, and was
induced to take up an allotment. I have been doing general
farming, and have been very successful. I had no capital

when I came here. All the cash I had was $1.50, although I had my team and waggon. I have paid the Army about $800 on land and stock, but yet owe them $1,094. My farm, stock, etc., I consider worth at least $3,000, so that I have made in the six years $2,000 clear. My land has recently been appraised at $100 per acre, but I would not like to take that amount for it. I am glad I came here for I have learned things about farming that I never knew before, and I believe I would make a success if I took a settlement in Siberia.

I have nineteen head of cattle, three mules and one colt. When the drainage in progress is finished it will make a great improvement, and the prospects should be very bright here. Personally I am doing well. I believe my next two crops of alfalfa, seed, and hay will enable me to clear off the balance owing the Army with all interest.

BENJAMIN MORRIS :—

(Renter.)

I have been here two years ; came from Hobart, Oklahoma, where I went at the time the place was opened for settlement by the Government. I failed to get a homestead and I came here. I have not purchased my farm. Am simply renting from the Army. The Army supplied me with cows, etc. I did very well last year, and expect to do much better this. I like Amity principally for the schools, etc., for the children, of which I have nine. The prospects here are very favourable. I do not consider the alkali serious, and feel sure that with a little draining it will be all right. My specialities are beets, grain, oats, wheat, alfalfa and vegetables ; in fact, general gardening. I consider that the Army is doing a good thing for poor people in colonising like this.

A. K. DURAND :—

I have been here five months ; came from New York City ; have farmed previously for a short time in Kansas. This year I am putting in about 40 acres of sugar beet, between 40 and 50 of oats, and will cut 90 acres of alfalfa and plant 10 acres of corn. I like the Colony very much, and think that my prospects for this year are very good.

JAMES H. CHILDS :—

Valuation . . .	$5,875 (or about)	£1,175
Amount owing Salvation Army and others	3,500 ,,	700
Equity . .	$2,375 ,,	£475

I was one of the first pioneers, having come from Chicago. Before leaving I worked as a check clerk for the C. and A. Railway. I am married and have nine children. All things considered I think I have done well. Two of my daughters have got married to good husbands, and my family and myself are all in good health.

As to how I have come out financially, I don't think I have any reason to complain. I came to years of maturity in the city and found myself never able to earn more than just sufficient to keep my family, with the exception of a house worth $1,000. Now, in addition to being my own boss, and living under healthy and pleasant conditions, I consider I am worth $6,525. This, of course, includes what I have got in my grocery store. After having lived on the Colony from the start, and being thoroughly acquainted with the Army's plan of colonising city people, I think it is fine from every standpoint. In fact, given good land, it simply cannot fail, because I know from experience the cities are full of people who are just longing for such a chance to acquire a home, but cannot get one, because they have not money to buy, and nobody but the Army is willing to trust them.

NOTE.—The equity quoted above evidently does not include Mr. Child's grocery store and the stock therein.—H. R. H.

JAMES MITCHELL :—

Valuation . . .	$1,409 (or about)	£281
Amount owing Salvation Army and others . .	735 ,,	147
Equity . .	$674 ,,	£134

I have been a colonist five years. Am married with one child. When I first located I had some stock, and some

7

horses worth, altogether, about $200. I now consider myself worth nearly a thousand dollars. I think well of the Colony plan.

GEORGE H. THOMAS :—

Valuation	.	. $5,700 (or about) £1,140		
Amount owing Salvation				
Army and others	.	2,723	,,	545
Equity .	. $2,977	,,	£595

I am one of the pioneer colonists, having landed here seven years ago. I came from Chicago. Am married, and have four children. I had about $300 to start with, but now consider myself to be worth about $3,000 over and above all my liabilities. I am more than glad I came here, and look forward with certainty to doing even better in the future. I like the country, the climate, and the people, and wish many of my Chicago friends could be given the chance of coming here. I have a good farm and a good grocery business, and besides, have just been elected Sheriff of this County, at a salary of about $1,800 a year.

You may be interested to know that I used to be a member of the London Metropolitan Police Force, under Commissioner Sir Charles Warren.

C. A. ERICKSON :—

Valuation	.	. $3,125 (or about) £625		
Amount owing Salvation				
Army and others .	.	2,199	,,	439
Equity .	.	$926	,,	£186

I came here from Chicago six years ago. Before coming I worked at tailoring, receiving a salary barely sufficient to keep my family. Here I consider I have done very well, for in addition to having paid all the expenses connected with the maintenance of my family I have accumulated an equity of at least $2,000. In fact, I would refuse that even

if offered in spot cash. I have got a valuable farm, and my
little coal business is steadily growing in value. Since I
only had $50 when I landed, and am a man of advanced
years, I consider that a pretty good showing, and all through
the generous help of the Salvation Army, without which help
I never should have got a home of my own; instead I should
still be stitching away in a close room in Chicago. I would
also like to say that life in the country has very much improved the health of myself and family. God bless the
Colony plan!

NOTE.—When Mr. Erickson estimates his equity at
$2,000 he probably includes the value of his coal busi-
ness.—H. R. H.

DOCTOR WILLIAM S. GREENARD, M.D. :—

Valuation . . .	$2,660 (or about)	£532
Amount owing Salvation Army and others . .	2,357 ,,	471
Equity . .	$303 ,,	£61

I own a farm on the Colony which I bought from a
colonist who had built up a grocery business in Amity, and
wanted to devote all his time to it. I bought it at the
rate of $115 per acre with improvements, but the colonist
from whom I bought it got it from the Army for $26, without
improvements, of course.

The object of my purchasing this property was because
I thought it a nice place for a home, and it presented good
opportunities for profitable farming; in fact, I looked on it
as a good, safe investment. I purchased this over a year
ago, and am glad I did so; in fact, I would be glad to buy
more land here at the same price.

I do not, of course, need any assistance from the Army
myself, but I look on the Army's plan of helping poor people
to acquire homes as a splendid one, and think the plan
could be made to work on a very large scale. I only wish
the Army had enough capital to plant a thousand people
where now there is only one.

NOTE.—There is a discrepancy between the amounts
given in the statement signed by Dr. Greenard and in those

7 *

shown against his name in the Financial Statement. A mistake must have been made in one or the other.—H. R. H.

LOUIS H. KEPHART :—

Valuation . . .	$4,060 (or about)	£812
Amount owing Salvation Army and others .	2,800 ,,	560
Equity . .	$1,260 ,,	£252

I am at present a farmer living in this region. I have just purchased 40 acres of Colony land at $70 per acre. I have bought it because I like the community, the absence of liquor and good moral surroundings in general. I also think it presents opportunity to make more than a good living, the land being located so close to the railroad tract, affording excellent opportunities for sheep raising, which industry I intend to continue to pursue.

ROBERT NEWMAN :—

Valuation . . .	$3,055 (or about)	£611
Amount owing Salvation Army and others .	1,628 ,,	325
Equity . .	$1,427 ,,	£286

I am married and have one girl, who has since married a colonist, and is doing very well. I have been a resident of the Colony for six years. Before coming here I was a carpenter and contractor in Chicago. I came here because my son had been located as a colonist, and thought I could do just as well on a farm as I could in a city. I had been raised on a farm. I had some capital when I came, amounting to about $600, and all considered I have done fairly well. After reckoning all my debts, am sure I am worth $2,000, and would not take a cent less if offered spot cash to-morrow. If I had been a young man I know I should have done much better ; with such a chance as the Army gives any good man ought to do well.

J. W. GARRISON :—

Valuation . . .	$2,969 (or about)	£594
Amount owing Salvation		
Army and others .	1,134 ,,	227
Equity . .	$1,835 ,,	£367

I do not consider myself exactly a colonist, but I have taken up Army lands a year ago, and the Army has helped to buy stock and implements with which to run my farm. Before coming here, I had bad luck, and in consequence had nothing but a team of horses. Now, I figure I am worth over $300 more than I was at that time, and I am getting fixed so as to do very much better in the future.

The Army has helped me to get everything I have. They have trusted as nobody else would, and I shall see that their confidence is not misplaced by paying back every dollar it has advanced me.

I think this Colony scheme the greatest thing in the world to help a man who wants to help himself.

No. 22.

State of Colorado, ⎫ ss.
County of Prowers. ⎭

F. de la Tour Booth Tucker and Alfred Hamon, being duly sworn, depose and say that the figures given in the attached statement are a true and correct abstract of the financial condition of the Salvation Army Colony known as Fort Amity, and situated in Prowers County, Colorado, U.S.A., as shown by the books of the Salvation Army, and statement of values given by a disinterested and reliable appraiser, duly sworn.

F. DE L. BOOTH TUCKER   (L.S.).
ALFRED HAMON   (L.S.).

Subscribed and sworn to before me, this 7th day of April, A.D. 1905.

W. A. French,   (L.S.)
Notary Public.

(Commission expires 21st February, 1907.)

No. 23.

State of Colorado, ⎫ SS.
County of Prowers. ⎭

I, Joseph S. McMurtry, Manager of the Holly Bank of Holly, Colorado, being duly sworn do hereby depose and state that the attached schedule of property owned by the Salvation Army and the members of the Fort Amity, Salvation Army Colony, is a full, true and correct statement of the property appraised by me this day, and that to the best of my knowledge and belief the values of the property therein given, to wit: one hundred and fifty-four thousand seven hundred and seventy-five ($154,775) dollars for land and improvements, and thirty thousand five hundred and sixty-four ($30,564) dollars for live stock and farming equipment, represents the true market value of the property listed.

(Signed)   JOSEPH S. McMURTRY.

Subscribed and sworn to before me this 7th day of April,
A.D. 1905.

(Signed)   JAMES B. HARDEN,
Notary Public.

(My Commission expires 20th January, 1907.)

(L.S.)

No. 24.

THE SALVATION ARMY.

Fort Amity Colony, Amity, Colorado, U.S.A.

Statements showing the financial position of the Colony on 1st April, 1905 (not including colonists' holdings), as per valuations made by J. S. McMurtry, Manager of the Holly Bank, of Holly, Colorado, and duly sworn to.

Assets.

	$	$
Land and Land Improvements :—		
Entire Colony, as per appraised valuation.	154,775.00	
Less value of land, etc., sold to colonists	66,530.00	
		88,245.00
Sanatorium Building . . .		20,500.00
Live stock and farming equipment	30,564.00	
Less value owned by colonists .	28,364.00	
		2,200.00
Furniture and fixtures :—		
In staff quarters and office . .		1,133.87
Colonists' indebtedness to Salvation Army :—		
For land, buildings, outfit loans, etc. (1st October, 1904) . .		54,887.96
Sundry debtors		157.60
Cash on hand		983.96
		168,108.39
Loss : Being net cost of management, including salaries of Colony staff, instructors, grants and rebates to colonists, interests on loan ($25,162.02), and all running expenses of the Colony for seven years		23,111.50
		$191,219.89
		(£38,243)

INFANTS' SCHOOL, FORT AMITY.

TOWN SITE STORES, FORT AMITY.

Liabilities.

The Salvation National Headquarters
   Loan for the purchase of land and
   the establishment and maintenance
   of the Colony 169,853.52
Loans for Sanatorium   .   .   . 20,958.49
                     ——————— 190,812.01
Sundry creditors 407.88
                                  $191,219.89
                                (£38,243)

No. 25.

THE SALVATION ARMY.

Fort Amity Colony, Amity, Colorado, U.S.A.

Statement showing financial condition of the Colony on 1st April, 1905, as per valuation made by J. S. McMurtry, Manager of the Holly Bank, of Holly, Colorado, and duly sworn to.

Assets.

	$	$
Land and Land Improvements :—		
Including cost of preparing land for irrigation, ditches, irrigation system, fencing, trees, dwellings, store buildings, barns, etc., and artesian well	154,775.00	
Sanatorium building . . .	20,500.00	
		175,275.00
Live stock :—		
Horses, cows, stock cattle, hogs, sheep, poultry and bees . .		10,872.00
Farming equipment :—		
Vehicles, harness, mowers and haying tools, harrows, ploughs, cream separators, incubators, tools, etc.		19,692.00
		$205,839.00
		(£41,167)

Liabilities.

	$	$
The Salvation Army National Head- quarters :—		
Loans for the purchase of land and the establishment and main- tenance of the Colony . .	169,853.52	
Loans for Sanatorium . . .	20,958.49	
		190,812.01
Surplus of assets over liabilities .		15,026.99
		$205,839.00
		(£41,167)

Note.—The Town site land has been valued on the same basis as the poorest agricultural areas, *viz.*, $60 per acre, and no cognizance has been taken of its special value for business purposes. Lots containing one-twelfth of an acre are at the present time selling at from $50 to $600 each.

No. 26.

SHORT HISTORIES OF THE AMITY COLONISTS.

BARKMAN.—From Kansas City. Married. Five children. Worked in packing house as meat-washer at $6.00 per week. Salvation Army paid his car fare out here.

CLOUGHLEY.—From Omaha, Nebraska. Married. Five children. Steam-fitter. Had $300.00 capital at starting.

COKER. — From Chicago. Married. Four children. Painter. No capital. Salvation Army paid his car fare.

COX.—From Chicago. Married. Two children. Teamster. No capital. Salvation Army paid car fare.

DAVY.—From Kansas City. Unmarried. No capital.

DOBLE.—From Sioux City, Nebraska. Married. Four children. Tinner by trade. No capital. Salvation Army paid his car fare.

ERIK ERICKSON.—From Chicago. Married. One child. Street car conductor. No capital. Salvation Army paid his car fare.

C. A. ERICKSON.—From Chicago. Married. Four children. Tailor. No capital. Salvation Army paid his car fare.

FREWING. — From Chicago. Married. Six children. Plasterer. No capital. Salvation Army paid his car fare.

GAYLORD.—From Chicago. Married. Three children. Photographer's canvasser. No capital.

GRINDROD.—From St. Joseph, Montana. Married. Eight children. Labourer in packing house. No capital. Car fare furnished by people interested in his case.

HARRIS.—Lived in this district. Unmarried. Had a team of horses and a few implements.

HARGREAVES.—From Philadelphia. Married. Three children. Salvation Army Officer. No capital. Salvation Army paid car fare.

INMAN.—Lived in this region. Married. Five children. No capital aside from his team.

KEPHART.—Lived in this region. A sheep raiser by profession, and located in order that he might teach this industry to the colonists. Has sufficient capital of his own.

McABEE.—From Alliance, Ohio. Married. One child. Grocery clerk. No capital. Salvation Army paid car fare.

MANNING.—Lived in this district, and located on the Colony because of his ability as a sugar beet grower. Had some horses and implements when located.

MITCHELL.—Lived in this district. Married. Very little capital.

J. H. NEWMAN.—From Chicago. Married. Three children. Carpenter. No capital. Salvation Army paid car fare.

R. NEWMAN.—From Chicago. Married. One child. Had $50 capital.

NICOL.—From Chicago. Married. Four children. Carpenter. No capital.

PRIEBE.—From Cleveland. Married. One child. Labourer. No capital. Salvation Army paid car fare.

PRINGLE.—From Hennessey, Oklahoma. Married. Three children. Land agent. Had $1,700 capital. Located because he was an expert fruit grower.

ROMIG.—From Medicine Lodge, Kansas. Married. Three children. Blacksmith.

SACHTLER.—From South Norwalk, Connecticut. Married. Eight children. Iron-moulder. No capital. Salvation Army paid car fare.

STEVENS.—Married. Three children. Salvation Army Officer. Had a team of horses.

STIMSON.—Lived in this district, and was located as a "pace setter". Had sufficient capital to pay for his place.

THOMAS.—From Chicago. Married. Four children. Had $300.00 capital. Was a teamster and furniture remover.

ZIEGLER.—From Sioux City, Iowa. Married. One child. Salesman. No capital.

WAIDNER.—From Baltimore. Married. One child. Labourer in packing house. No capital. Salvation Army paid his car fare.

GARRISON.—From Syracuse, Kansas. Married. Three children. Farmer, without a farm; he did, however, have a team of horses.

MORRIS.—From Oklahoma. Married. Seven children. Cow-boy. No capital.

CHILDS.—From Chicago. Married. Nine children. Checker for the C. and A. Railroad Co., at a salary of $12.00 per week. Owned a house worth $1,000.00.

No. 27.

STATEMENT SHOWING THE FINANCIAL POSITION OF THE COLONISTS (NOT INCLUDING "RENTERS") ON THE SALVATION ARMY FORT AMITY COLONY, 4TH APRIL, 1905.

Name.	Land, Building and Improvement.	Live Stock.	Farming Equipment, etc.	Total.	Amount Owing to Salvation Army.	Other Liabilities.	Total Liabilities.	Total Equity.	Remarks.
	Dols.	Dols.	Dols.	Dols.	Dols.	Dols.	Dols.	Dols.	
Backman	1560	700	175	2435	1814.41	100	1914.41	520.00	
Coker	2640	150	750	3540	1326.67	—	1326.67	2213.33	Had 13 dols. to commence with.
Childs	2700	125	3050	5875	1700.00	1800	3500.00	2375.00	Had 1000 dols. to commence with.
Cox	1860	100	80	2040	1759.35	100	1859.35	180.65	
Cloughley	1925	240	150	2315	1618.29	—	1618.29	696.71	
Davy	2585	50	350	2985	904.28	—	904.28	2080.72	
Doble	1835	900	190	2925	1927.72	111	2038.72	886.28	Had 10 dols. to commence.
Erickson, E.	1680	500	315	2495	1901.78	10	1911.78	583.22	Had 25 dols. to commence.
Erickson, C. A.	2340	35	750	3125	1499.96	700	2199.96	925.04	Had 20 dols. to commence.
Frewing	2440	75	100	2615	1618.93	—	1618.93	996.07	
Greenard	2900	—	—	2900	2107.37	—	2107.37	792.63	
Grindrod	1715	800	145	2660	2332.47	25	2357.47	302.53	
Gaylord	1885	200	135	2220	1555.00	—	1555.00	665.00	
Harris	2210	250	175	2635	1080.76	—	1080.76	1554.24	Had team and waggon
Hargreaves	2685	300	200	3185	1831.50	—	1831.50	1353.50	
Inman	2112	325	85	2522	1892.10	62	1954.10	567.90	Had team and waggon
Kephart	4060	—	—	4060	2800.00	—	2800.00	1260.00	
Manning	2381	700	200	3281	1834.65	—	1834.65	1446.35	Had horses and cattle worth 350 dols.
McAbee	755	225	175	1155	1357.91	390	1747.91	—	
Mitchell	1049	260	100	1409	735.67	—	735.67	673.33	Had horses and cattle worth 700 dols.
Nicol	2108	300	90	2498	1806.40	35	1841.40	656.60	Had 25 dols.
Newman, H.	3085	170	4275	7530	1223.76	1000	2223.76	5306.24	Had 50 dols.
Newman, R.	1575	100	1380	3055	628.49	1000	1628.49	1426.21	Had 600 dols.
Priebe	1875	350	70	2295	2437.22	40	2477.22	—	Had 3 dols.
Pringle	1850	450	175	2475	1185.88	—	1185.88	1289.12	Had 1765 dols.
Stevens	2395	—	145	2540	764.84	—	764.84	1775.16	Had team and waggon
Sachtler	1870	250	150	2270	2160.91	125	2285.91	—	Had 25 dols.
Thomas	2790	325	2585	5700	1723.79	1000	2723.79	2976.21	Had 300 dols.
Waidner	1765	200	115	2080	2328.27	25	2353.27	—	
Ziegler	1700	1400	305	3405	1798.54	384	2182.54	1222.96	Had 125 dols.
Garrison	500	1192	1277	2969	934.00	200	1134.00	1835.00	Had live stock worth 300 dols.
Romig	1700	—	—	1700	1036.32	—	1036.32	663.68	
Dols.	66530	10672	17692	94894	51627.24	7107	58734.24	37223.68	
or £	13306	2134	3538	18978	10325	1421	11746	7444	

Note.—Average equity per colonist, 1163.00 dols. (or about £233).

No. 28.

MEMORANDUM OF INFORMATION RESPECTING THE SALVATION ARMY COLONY AT AMITY, PROWERS COUNTY, COLORADO.

LOCATION.

The Colony is situated 257 miles south and east of Denver, and 12 miles west of the Kansas line.   It is on the main line of the A. T. & S. F. Railroad, and has a depôt and express office.   The town, plotted two years ago, is building up, and has at the present time sixteen established businesses, among which are general merchants, hardware and boot and shoe stores, also blacksmith shops, drug store, livery stable, etc.

LAND.

The land formed a part of the famous Amity Land and Irrigation Company's enterprise, and it is of a rich alluvial loam, which, when put into cultivation and properly looked after, yields abundantly.

AMOUNT ALLOTTED AND PRICE.

Twenty acres of land are allotted to each colonist, every purchaser being allowed to make his own choice of location. Price of land without improvements at this date ranges from $50.00 to $75.00 per acre, including a sufficient water right deeded in perpetuity.

WATER SUPPLY AND IRRIGATION.

Water for irrigation is obtained from the Buffalo canal, one of the best and surest flowing ditches in Colorado. Fifty cents per acre is charged annually by the water company for the maintenance of the canal.

Main laterals, costing several thousands of dollars, have been constructed by the Army; the cost of these is included in the price of the land.   Each colonist constructs the distributing ditches on his own farm.   The main laterals are

kept in repair jointly by the farmers who draw their supply
through the same.

The practice of irrigation is comparatively simple and
easily understood and does not require any very special skill
on the part of the irrigator.   A bulletin issued by the Department of Agriculture at Washington, No. 73, "Irrigation in
the Rocky Mountain States," furnishes information in ele-
mentary form concerning this subject.

BUILDINGS.

The Salvation Army makes a cash loan not to exceed
$300.00 with which to purchase sufficient material for a
good substantial house and barn.   Colonists are expected
to construct their own buildings, but where they are not
capable of doing so, the Army will agree to $25.00 of the
above $300.00 being spent in the hire of mechanics to do
any difficult work which the colonist cannot undertake alone.

Buildings must be of stone, but good rock can be obtained
within half a mile of the colony at $2.50 per cord of 100
square feet, loaded on the waggon.

Colonists can suit themselves as to the style of house, but
plans must be passed by the manager.

OUTFIT.

To colonists unable to purchase them, the Army furnishes
a team of horses, implements, cow, seed, etc.   Work can
usually be got by those who desire it, to provide groceries,
etc., till the first crop is harvested.

TERMS.

On land and buildings twelve years' time is given, subject to a contract which will be sent to colonists at the
time of their acceptance.   For the first two years interest
only is expected.   Afterwards, one-tenth of total cost each
year, with interest at 6 per cent. till the whole is paid.
Loans for live stock and equipment are secured by chattel
mortgage, and are payable in five equal annual instalments,
with interest at 6 per cent.

CROPS.

Among our staple crops are sugar beets, which produce from seven to fifteen tons to the acre, according to the care taken of them, and sell to the sugar factory at from $4.00 to $6.00 per ton. Rocky Ford cantaloupes are also extensively grown and are usually quite profitable; moreover, the colony possesses exceptional possibilities for dairying and hog raising, the alfalfa pasture making excellent forage. Of fruits: apples, peaches, cherries and plums do well, and we believe small fruits can be made a great success.

We do not, however, recommend colonists to put all their eggs into one or two baskets, but urge them to diversify, especially seeing to it that everything required for the sustenance of themselves and stock is provided for. "Never sending a dollar off the farm for what the farm will produce" should be the motto of every settler.

MARKETS.

Denver and other market towns make good outlets for all kinds of produce. Kansas City is not much farther from us, and can take care of a large amount of our goods.

CLIMATE.

The climate of Colorado is a most desirable and healthy one. All our colonists have been benefited by coming here, especially those suffering from weak lungs. The air is light and bracing, and though the summer days are hot, the nights are always delightfully cool. Sunstrokes are said to be unknown in the State. The average winters are mostly mild and open, though at times the cold snaps are severe.

GENERAL.

Good stock water can be had anywhere on the colony at about ten feet. For family drinking water, however, we recommend that from the artesian well recently sunk on the town site, at a cost of $1,200. Each colonist is obligated to buy a share in this. The price is $15.00, payable in three equal annual instalments.

8

Social and Educational.

The colony is not in any sense intended for Salvationists only; in fact, the majority of residents here are not members of the organisation; we have, however, a properly organised Salvation Army Corps, under the leadership of an experienced officer. Two week-night meetings and several meetings on Sunday are open to all who wish to attend, as well as a carefully superintended Sunday School for the children.

The colonists meet as often as practicable for the discussion of topics relating to farming, irrigation, etc., and, as often as circumstances will permit, Farmers' Institutes are conducted by the Faculty of the State Agricultural College.

Our schools are good, and our district contains more children of school age than any other district in the county, except the county seat. A new school-house has just been completed, at a cost of $2,500, and four teachers engaged for the coming winter.

Miscellaneous.

We have a post office, with both domestic and foreign money order branches.

Our population at the time of writing is about 300.

The Salvation Army Cherry Tree Orphanage, costing $20,000, is located here, and is said to be the finest building in the country. It has accommodation for from eighty to one hundred children.[1]

Two doctors reside on the ground.

Finally.

It is well for the colonists to understand that they are starting life in a new country, and must come expecting to do exactly as the pioneer has always been compelled to do, namely, to work long hours and endure some privation for the first year or two. This is a strong man's proposition, and wives and children must unite their efforts in the fields with their husbands and fathers in the struggle to pay for a home.

---

[1] This is now a Sanatorium for Consumptives.—H. R. H.

No. 29.

REMARKS ON THE FORT HERRICK COLONY
OF THE SALVATION ARMY.

1. Fort Herrick, the third of the Salvation Army Land
Colonies in the United States, which I was directed to
inspect, is situated in the township of Mentor, about twenty
miles from the City of Cleveland, in Ohio, wherewith it is
connected by a tramway that reaches it from Cleveland in
one hour and a half, and also by railway lines that run
through vineyards and orchard lands. It has an area of
some 280 acres of land, of which about 40 are under wood.
When I visited it on the 10th of April, 1905, the trees were not
yet out, and the only crops visible above the ground were
wheat and clover. Still, the situation of the place struck me as
pretty, consisting, as it does, of a stretch of flat ground, almost
entirely surrounded by native timber. Doubtless this land at
some time or other was covered with the waters of Lake Erie.

2. Briefly, this is the history of the Fort Herrick Colony :—
In the year 1899 the Honourable Myron T. Herrick, the
present Governor of Ohio, whose invitation to stay with
him at Columbus I was exceedingly sorry to be forced by
circumstances to decline, and Mr. James Parmolco, a citizen
of Cleveland, presented the land to the Salvation Army,
who at first seem to have contemplated the establishment
of a settlement there upon the pattern of those at Fort
Romie and Fort Amity. Indeed, a start was made in this
direction, eight or nine families being put upon the land.
It was soon found, however (as here irrigation is not practised), that each family required more ground than was
available. At first the Authorities of the Salvation Army
purposed adding to their area, but this idea they were
obliged to abandon, as land adjoining Fort Herrick is very
expensive, and funds were not forthcoming to purchase
more. The end of it was, therefore, that the settlement
plan was given up, and the families who had already come
there were provided for in various ways. One went to Fort
Romie and one to Fort Amity, while another remained at
Fort Herrick, and others found farms or employment in the
neighbourhood.

8 *

3. It must, therefore, be clearly understood that Fort Herrick is in no sense a land settlement Colony, nor does it throw any direct light upon the problems on which I am directed to report.

4. Having abandoned their plan of using this place as a land settlement, it occurred to the Salvation Army Authorities that its pleasant and convenient situation made it very suitable for the purpose of the establishment of a small industrial Colony of an agricultural character, somewhat similar in nature to that at Hadleigh, in England, of which a description will be found in an appendix to my report.

One of the objects of this Colony, therefore, is more or less to "agriculturise" certain of the city institutions of the Salvation Army, it being intended to transplant thither in process of time some of the semi-charitable sections of their work in the United States, and thus to give the inmates of those sections the advantage of agricultural employment and instruction. It is thought, also, that those of them who may be suitable might afterwards be drafted to regular land settlements, and there started upon an independent career.

5. A commencement has been made in the direction indicated above by the establishment at Fort Herrick of an Inebriates' Home. Major McFee, the manager, informed me that sixty inebriates, taken from the cities, had, up to the date of my visit, passed through this home, during the preceding four months, that is to the 1st of January, and are now, all of them, in good employment. Several of these men also are at work upon the Colony itself, where I saw and spoke with some of them, to all appearance very respectable persons.

6. This success struck me as so remarkable that I enquired into the causes of it, and found that there is no drinking saloon within nine miles of the Colony, as, under an exercise of what is known as "local option," this is what is called a "dry district"; that is, drink cannot be purchased within its limits. Here, it is probable, we have one of the main causes of this sudden access of sobriety among those who, in the immediate past, have been complete strangers to that virtue. Others are, as the sufferers themselves admit, the country air, which appears to take away their desire for spirituous liquors, and the escape from city life, with its ever-present degradations and temptations.

7. However these things may be, that the Inebriates' Home at Fort Herrick does a good work there can be no doubt. Thus, for example, one man there, who a year ago was taken from the workhouse—an institution that in the United States partakes of the nature of a penitentiary—has, out of his small pay, now accumulated a banking account which amounts to $60.

8. It is also purposed, when the funds are available, to establish here a home for orphans with a view of their being trained in agriculture. Further, a leading object of the colony is to experiment on certain agricultural lines in order to gain experience which can be made use of at the land settlements. Thus, the breeding of pigeons, which are known locally as "squabs," and the sale of their young upon the market, has already been undertaken with good success. An apiary, too, has been started, and there is an idea of setting up the industry of the making of hives, which would give employment to many of the unfortunate persons with whom the Salvation Army has to deal.

9. It will be seen, therefore, that this enterprise, although entirely distinct from its land settlements proper and at present largely of a charitable character, is a not unimportant branch of the Army's work in the United States, where it is destined to form the natural connecting link between their city institutions and their land settlements.

10. Some short account of the system of farming practised at Fort Herrick may be of interest. The soil consists of about eight inches of loam on red clay, which in turn lies upon a porous white clay. It is fairly easy to work if treated at the proper time, but requires manure and dressings of lime to correct the natural acidity.

A four-course shift is followed: the clover ley after being ploughed in is succeeded by maize, then come oats, then wheat, with which clover and other grass seeds are sown. The manure is applied for the wheat, and, if available, for the oats as well. Barley, rye and peas are also grown, but from the plant of it which I saw upon the ground, I should judge that here wheat is as reliable a crop as any. Cows and stock are kept, and with these many miscellaneous creatures, some of them not usually found upon a farm,

Thus, there are the pigeons, or squabs, already mentioned, which seem to be doing extremely well, a fair-sized apiary of Italian bees—then just beginning their season's work—turkeys, Pekin ducks, fowls of various sorts, a few pheasants, of the kind that we shoot in England, for which there is now a considerable demand in the United States, and, lastly, some Southern bloodhounds, which find a market here, to be used, I understand, in the tracking of criminals.

11. I walked all over this farm and into the woods with which it is bordered, where the principal timbers are oak, two kinds of maple, ash, sycamore, and bass wood. The land, which is rather liable to hold the water, is drained by open ditches and not with tiles.

12. At one corner of the place, upon a rising meadow, by which flows a stream, I saw the site of the future Agricultural Training School, which struck me as well chosen.

13. A few small pieces of land have been sold off by the Army to cottagers in order to encourage their settlement upon the place. Thus, I visited the house of a Dane, named Greeshange, who has a wife and a family of six bright-looking children. To this man the Army has sold two and a half acres at the rate of $100 per acre, which purchase price he is allowed to pay off in $10 monthly instalments. By working for the Army upon the farm he can earn $35 per month, out of which the $10 due from him on account of the land purchased are stopped. I quote the instance as it struck me as a good way of enabling such people to become the owners of a piece of land, that is where work is available and their labour is desired.

14. It should be remembered, however, that in this part of the United States agricultural hands seem to be scarce. At least, Major McFee informed me that he had applications from neighbouring farmers for the next twenty inebriates that he could turn out as cured.

I do not append any individual statements to these remarks as I have done in the cases of Fort Romie and Fort Amity, since there are no colonists proper at Fort Herrick from whom to take them, and those of the inebriates would scarcely be of value.

H. RIDER HAGGARD,
Commissioner.

No. 30.

FORT HERRICK COLONY.

9th April, 1905.

NOTES OF AN INTERVIEW between Commissioner H. RIDER
HAGGARD and Commander BOOTH TUCKER.   The following
persons were also present, *viz.*, Colonel Higgins, Mr. Ranson Caygill, Miss Angela R. Haggard, and Mr. Harry Wright.

The conversation was opened by the Commissioner, who
asked Commander Booth Tucker the following question :—

Q. Will you please describe this colony?

A. Commander Booth Tucker: Fort Herrick is situated
in the township of Mentor, about 20 miles from the city
of Cleveland, in Ohio, and consists of about 280 acres ; about
40 acres of wooded land and the balance agricultural.   It is
watered by natural rainfall.

Q. I want you to tell me the history of the Fort Herrick
Colony, or Institution.

A. Commander Booth Tucker : A short time after we
had started our colonies in Colorado and California, about
July, 1899, we were offered a piece of land by the Honourable Myron T. Herrick, the present Governor of Ohio, and
Mr. James Parmelee, a prominent citizen of Cleveland.   It
was first intended to add to this adjoining land, but the
price proved to be prohibitive and the funds for such exten-
sion unavailable.   Moreover, the farm was of an extremely
valuable character and peculiarly well suited by its situation
for the establishment of some of the Salvation Army charitable Institutions.   We felt, therefore, that it would be a
pity to part with the ownership of the land, so we determined to reserve it to serve as a connecting link between
the city Institutions and our land settlements.   We are,
therefore, at present, utilising it for this purpose.

Q. Have you any settlers there at all?

A. Commander Booth Tucker: There are no settlers
there, strictly speaking.   The whole institution is under
the management of Major and Mrs. McFee, who see to
the cultivation of the land and who are also responsible for
the management of the small Inebriates' Home which we

have established upon it, and for certain agricultural experiments which we are making.

Q. Did you ever have any settlers there?

A. Commander Booth Tucker: Yes; we had some eight or nine families. One of the difficulties we experienced was that owing to the fact that the land was not irrigated they wanted more land than we were able to give them in such an expensive location.

Q. What became of them?

A. Commander Booth Tucker: Two of them went to our Colonies; one to Fort Romie and one to Fort Amity.

Q. And of the others?

A. Commander Booth Tucker: They have been provided for in various ways. To some of them Fort Herrick has proved a stepping-stone to better opportunities. For instance, two sisters had a fine farm on the adjoining hills, and took one of our best families into partnership with them. Another landowner in the neighbourhood sold to one of the colonists a nice farm, with a comfortable house upon it, to be paid for in instalments.

Q. So they all went away?

A. Commander Booth Tucker: Yes; they were all looked after in one way or another.

Q. Then did the experiment as a settlement come to an end?

A. Commander Booth Tucker: Yes; about two years ago.

Q. Did you incur any considerable loss over it?

A. Commander Booth Tucker: Only those expenses incidental to the improvement of the land, of which the value now remains.

Q. Then after that was the Colony started on a new basis as an industrial settlement?

A. Commander Booth Tucker: Yes; that is so. Our intention is to place some of our other Institutions there, as we get the funds to pay for the necessary buildings. For instance, we want to train children in agriculture, and propose to start a children's home for that purpose.

Q. What is there then at the present moment?

A. Commander Booth Tucker: We are experimenting there along certain agricultural lines, with a view to introducing them on our settlements if the experiments prove satisfactory, ultimately making the place self-supporting

upon an agricultural basis. For instance, we have introduced there the "squab" industry, that is the growing of
young pigeons for the market. This is reckoned to be a
very paying business. Then, again, we have poultry and
a few pheasants, for which there is a great demand in some
parts of the country. Then we have a dairy business also,
and we hope to manufacture bee-hives.

Q. How is the place supported; out of the General Funds
of the Army?

A. Commander Booth Tucker: It is partially supported
by the dairy, the sale of poultry and so forth, for which
there is a great demand in the neighbourhood.

Colonel Higgins: At the present time the Salvation Army
Industrial Homes Company (Incorporated) runs the Fort
Herrick Farm for the Salvation Army, and the Company
stands whatever loss is incurred from its working.

Q. Well, it is clearly not a colony, so I suppose there is
nothing more to say about it?

A. Commander Booth Tucker: No; it is not. It is intended to serve the same purpose as a number of similar
Institutions which we have scattered through the world.
For instance, we have a "Prison Gate" Home at Colombo,
Ceylon, for ex-criminals, whom we train in agriculture, and
a similar institution in Cape Town, South Africa, in both of
which we have dairy cows, and supply the cities with milk
to help to meet the expenses of the home.

The Commissioner: Thank you, gentlemen.

> H. Rider Haggard, Commissioner.
> F. Booth Tucker, Commander.
> Ed. Jno. Higgins, Chief Secretary.
> Jos. R. McFee, Fort Herrick Manager.

No. 31.

SS. *Majestic*,
20th April, 1905.

SIR,

REFERRING to our various conversations and to the interview that I had the pleasure of holding with you and other officers of the Salvation Army at Fort Amity, Colorado, U.S.A., on the 5th April, 1905, on which occasion you assured me on behalf of the Salvation Army that, in the event of the provision of the necessary capital, your Organisation would be willing to undertake "to any extent" its application in the selection of suitable persons to place upon the land, and the management of such settlements on a large scale, I have now the honour to ask you for your formal assurances in writing in confirmation of these statements that I may convey the same to His Majesty's Government.

I think it my duty to ask you also what guarantee you are in a position to give to His Majesty's Government that the policy of the Salvation Army in this matter will be continuous, and what arrangements your Organisation has made to insure its permanence as a social and charitable Institution.

It has occurred to me that this latter question may involve the revealing of matters which the Salvation Army considers as private to itself. In that event I shall be prepared to treat them as confidential, and humbly to request His Majesty's Government to do the same.

It will be obvious to you that I cannot in justice ask the Government to consent to the handling by your Organisation of considerable sums of money and to its exercise of administrative authority over large land settlements, such as I have in view, unless these points are made clear beyond all possibility of ambiguous interpretation or of doubt.

I have also to ask you whether the Salvation Army would be prepared to work with and under the supervision of an Imperial official, to be appointed by the Government, to be known as the Superintendent of Land Settlements or by some similar title.

Should the Government see fit to appoint such an officer, his duties, I imagine, would include the allocation of funds for the forming and development of individual settlements, the right of inspection of such settlements at all times, the prevention of the exercise of religious pressure in any shape upon the settlers or their children, the right to reject any settlers of whom he did not approve, and of submitting all accounts to a professional audit.

Lastly, I shall be glad to know whether the Salvation Army is prepared to undertake this important work for the sake of charity and for the general good of our Country and its Colonies alone, charging against the colonisation funds provided only the actual salaries paid to the managers of the Colonies and to their subordinates, or whether they would expect any pecuniary return for their labours?

I am, Sir,
Yours very truly,
H. RIDER HAGGARD,
Commissioner.

To Commander Booth Tucker,
  of the Salvation Army.

No. 32.

SS. Majestic,
24th April, 1905.

SIR,

IN reply to the various questions contained in your letter dated 20th inst., I would beg to answer them in the affirmative.

In the event of the provision of the necessary capital, our Organisation will be prepared to undertake to any extent its application in the selection of suitable persons to place upon the land, and the management of such settlements on a large scale.

Humanly speaking, I believe that the policy of the Salvation Army in this matter will be continuous. Every possible arrangement has been made to ensure the permanence of the Salvation Army as a social and a charitable Institution.

Whilst thanking you for your offer to treat information upon this point as confidential, I have to assure you that we have no information to give upon the question which needs to be considered private. Arrangements have been made for the devolution of the leadership and the management of the Army of a nature which, so far as we can foresee, must ensure its permanence and that of its work upon the present established lines and basis.   These arrangements we shall be happy to explain to His Majesty's Government if it is so desired.

In the case of the appointment by His Majesty's Government of a Superintendent of Land Settlements, or other similar officer, we shall be perfectly prepared to work with and under his supervision, submitting all accounts to his inspection and inviting in all branches of the undertaking his counsel, scrutiny and co-operation.

Furthermore, the Salvation Army is prepared to undertake the work of land settlement anywhere within the boundaries of the British Empire for the sake of charity for the general good alone, charging against the colonisation funds only the actual salaries and out-of-pocket expenses paid to or by the managers of the colonies, their directors and subordinates, together with the cost of the dwellings occupied by the said managers and their assistants.

The Salvation Army would expect no other pecuniary return or remuneration of any sort for its labours in this cause.

I trust it may not be out of place to take this opportunity of thanking you on behalf of General Booth and the Salvation Army for the careful and exhaustive examination which you have made into our American Colonies.   Your labours have indeed been monumental.   No detail has been too trivial to escape your attention, and no toil too fatiguing for you to undertake.

I would thank you too for the valuable suggestions you have made.   We have been glad that your abundant stores of practical experience should have been brought to bear upon the elaboration of this enterprise, and we sincerely hope that you will continue to pass on any suggestions that may occur to you with the assurance that they will receive our careful attention.

To our colonists themselves, I can assure you, as well as to our managers, your visit has been an inspiration and encouragement, and I sincerely hope that the cause of colonisation may long continue to enjoy both the guidance

of your experienced hand and the advocacy of your eloquent
pen and tongue.

From the considerable knowledge which the leaders of our
Organisation possess as to the condition of the working
classes and as to the possibilities of colonisation under wise
management, we have every confidence in the practicability
of your proposals which you have been good enough to
explain to me.   It is, so far as I am aware, the first definite
business-like proposal that has yet been advanced for dealing
on a large and scientific basis with what is universally
admitted to be one of the most serious problems of the day.

Finally, I would venture to congratulate you on the remarkable success of your negotiations with the Canadian
Government.   That you should have been able to secure
from them so exceedingly liberal an offer of land seems to
me to augur well for the future success of your proposal.

The cordiality of your reception both in Canada and in
the United States, the keen interest with which your mission
was regarded by all sections of the public, the extensive
notices devoted to it in the daily papers, and the warm
sentiments of friendliness towards Great Britain that were
so spontaneously expressed, seem to indicate that the results
of your visit will be much more far-reaching and beneficial
than was originally contemplated.

Assuring you once more of our sincere appreciation of the
toil your mission has involved,

I am, Sir,

Yours very truly,

FREDERICK ST. G. BOOTH TUCKER.

To H. Rider Haggard, Esq.,
    Commissioner.

No. 33.

REMARKS ON THE HADLEIGH COLONY OF THE SALVATION ARMY IN ESSEX, ENGLAND.

1. In the month of February, 1905, I thoroughly inspected the Hadleigh Colony of the Salvation Army, which is situated on the banks of the Thames in Essex, 4 miles from Southend and 39 miles by road from London.

2. The Colony has an area of about 3,000 acres, whereof some 300 or 400 acres are at present let off to a farmer.

3. The land for the most part is a stiff clay, overlying beds of the London Clay. It is poor and cold in character. In fact, its nature can be very well observed in the course of a railway journey from London to Leigh Station. On either side of the line are thousands of acres of a similar quality, which doubtless once bore good crops of corn. Now, however, the most of it has gone down to wretched pasture of an utterly innutritious nature, much of which the owners or tenants do not even take the trouble to keep clear of brambles and other noxious growths.

Of such land as this has been formed the Hadleigh Colony with its 100 acres of fruit trees, its upland and marsh pastures, its brickworks and chicken farms, and its market garden, from which Colony the total receipts for 1904 amounted, I am informed, to over £33,000.

4. When the Salvation Army purchased the place in the year 1890, at an average cost of about £20 the acre, it consisted of three unoccupied farms, almost devoid of population. Now the population upon the same land, including the Salvation Army officials and their families and certain employees indirectly associated with the undertaking, numbers over 500 souls, and, including the cost of food and management expenses, about £180 per week is spent on labour. At the time of my visit also there were employed upon the Colony a further 200 persons, who had been sent thither by the Mansion House Relief Fund Committee.

5. As a result of the establishment of this Salvation Army settlement also, a village has sprung up at Hadleigh, numbering at least 1,300 souls. Thus the populating of empty land has in its turn created a village population.

6. The poor persons received upon the Hadleigh Colony are of three classes :—

(1) Those who are introduced through the agency of the Salvation Army Social Operations in various parts of England.

(2) Those who are sent there by various Poor Law Authorities, with which Authorities agreements have been made for the payment of varying sums on their account for fixed periods, such sums running from five shillings to ten shillings and sixpence per week for periods of from three to twelve months.

(3) Special cases introduced either by philanthropic Societies or by relatives or friends of persons desiring to receive the benefits of the Colony.

The first of these classes (Social Operations of the Salvation Army) are generally selected men who have expressed some desire to be trained in pursuits connected with the land. Usually these are persons who, though suffering from misfortune and untoward circumstances, are really anxious to work and recover their positions. In nearly all cases they have expressed a desire to go abroad if found suitable for emigration.

Class two, though sent by the Poor Law Authorities, are for the most part selected by officers of the Salvation Army Colony from among able-bodied paupers nominated by the Guardians. They are generally from twenty-five to forty years of age, and drawn from various classes, amongst them being labourers, artisans and, occasionally, professional men. These persons, although paupers, are for the most part respectable, anxious to improve their positions, and able to work.

The third class, namely those sent by philanthropic Societies and by relatives and friends, are generally weak and very unsatisfactory specimens of humanity, who, as a last resource, have sought the shelter of the Salvation Army.

7. The result of the employment of this class of labour is to make the working of the Colony very expensive, owing to the necessity there is of maintaining a number of persons who are practically " wastrels " and by no means pay for their keep. Hadleigh Colony, therefore, cannot be considered from the point of view of an ordinary commercial undertaking, as it partakes largely of the nature of a charity.

I understand, however, that the annual deficit, which in 1892 amounted to between £4,000 and £5,000, is now very small, and when the brickworks, etc., are fully developed there seems to be a probability that it will be wiped out altogether.

8. I have not gone into the finance of the place very thoroughly or obtained any independent valuations as I had no object in so doing, but I am informed that the total capital invested in the Colony is about £130,000. Of this amount about £70,000 is represented by the lands and buildings; £30,000 by the brickworks and other industries, and another £30,000 by stock and implements.

As in the case of those in the United States, this Colony was started without sufficient capital, with the result that it is mortgaged or otherwise forms the security for about £100,000, borrowed at 4 per cent. per annum to pay for it and to start the various industries, etc. Still, the financial position seems to be quite sound, as I am told and can well believe that at the present day it, and the industries connected with it, must be valued at well over £200,000. The result of its establishment upon land values in the immediate neighbourhood is certainly remarkable. Thus an adjoining property is, I was assured, being offered at £60 the acre, which in 1890 would have fetched much nearer £10 the acre.

9. From the ruins of Hadleigh Castle, where Anne Boleyn was imprisoned, I obtained a good view of the Hadleigh Colony. Beneath lay some 600 acres of marshes, part of the Salvation Army estate. These are used as grazing grounds to fatten stock in summer; also Shire horses are bred here. The marshes are bordered by an estuary of the Thames, known as "Hadleigh Ray," which belongs to the Army. Here is a wharf for loading and unloading barges, which is fitted with steam plant, but as yet no direct connection has been made between it and the London and Tilbury Railway.

Also there are six and a quarter miles of sea wall, which has an average height of sixteen feet and is built of clay and protected in places by stone facing and wooden piles. This wall has been heightened by the Army, and its upkeep is very expensive. Normally this costs about £200 a year, but in 1905, owing to the high tide of 30th December, 1904, it will cost £500. This tide also damaged 200 acres of marsh land by submerging it in salt water.

Hence also can be seen the short railway built by the Army which terminates at the wharf on the Ray, where all bricks produced upon the Colony are laden, and materials used, such as coals, manure, etc., are unloaded, Most of the manure, however, is brought from Southend at a cost of from three shillings and sixpence to five shillings per load. London manure delivered at the wharf only costs about three shillings per load. Still it comes more expensive than that which is purchased at Southend, as the haulage to the upland part of the Colony amounts to another three shillings per load.

10. Still looking from the Castle, I saw to the West No. 1 brickfield, that in February was not working. When in operation it has a possible output of 6,000,000 bricks per annum and an actual output of about 4,000,000.

11. To the east of this brickfield is a reservoir with a capacity of 1,250,000 gallons, which was in course of construction by the labour of men from various London Poor Law Unions. These men receive from sixpence to two shillings and sixpence per week and their food from the Salvation Army, which pays them in accordance with the value of their work.

Subsequently I visited both this brickfield and the reservoir, whereof the watershed is formed by the slopes of hills that rise on either side of a little valley which runs down to the Ray. At the foot of this valley is a deep ditch that carries much water in the winter and at any time of rain. This ditch was in course of being tapped about 150 yards above the reservoir which it will feed by means of cemented pipes. Two men were digging the pipe trench, a groom from Ireland and an engineer from London, who had lost their employment. They were doing their work very well. The dam, or reservoir, had been thirteen weeks in course of construction, and up to that time had cost about £150. It is a large triangular excavation, dug in firm clay, which will need no concrete or puddling at the bottom, although a little cementing may be necessary on the sides. The water stored here will be of benefit to the neighbouring brickworks.

12. One of the troubles with which the Salvation Army

9

has to deal at Hadleigh is a lack of water. Many thousands
of pounds have been spent on two artesian wells, the cheaper
of which cost £4,000 and is yielding 20,000 gallons a day,
which is as much as the present plant can lift. Even now
there is not sufficient water, but the new reservoir will help
matters in this respect.

13. On my way to the temporary dining hall I saw the
causeway or raised road which was made last year by the
help of unemployed labour from London. It is 250 yards
long and cost about £450, but the London Unemployed
Committee made a grant of £150 towards the work.

14. In the dining hall I found about 160 men at their
mid-day meal. First we visited the kitchen, which is fitted
with a steam-cooking apparatus. The food is distributed
by cooks, who serve out a liberal portion on a plate to
which are added parsnips, boiled potatoes and bread. Tea
is also given in large mugs, and the meat is followed by tart
or pudding. Three meals are furnished a day; the average
cost per head of feeding these men being about one shilling
and twopence per day, which suffices to provide them with
an ample supply of good and wholesome food. Some of the
men are fed rather more plentifully and better than others,
the supply being proportioned in accordance with their personal and physical character and that of the labour which
they do.

I tasted some of the food and found it excellent. The
dinner I have already described. For breakfast the fare
consists of a good-sized plate of oatmeal porridge, bread,
butter and tea, with corned beef or German sausage, and
for tea bread, butter, some fresh or preserved meat and
tea.

I spoke to several of the men and lads here and elsewhere.
In substance all their stories were very similar. Either they
had fallen out of work and were starving or they were wan-
dering about the streets, or they had "gone to the bad".
In every case the Salvation Army had picked them up, and
they assured me that they were happy and contented. As
a specimen I will quote an interview with one of the cooks.

Q. What were you before you came to the Colony?

A. Brushmaker in London, sir.

Q. Did you fall out of work?

A. Yes.

Q. Got in a bad way ?

A. I did, in London and around the country.

Q. The Salvation Army picked you up ?

A. They did.

Q. And you are now a cook here ? What do you look forward to doing ultimately ? Going out to be a cook ?

A. I want to go to Canada in the spring.

The men at work in this kitchen were a most respectable-looking set, but I was told that they all came to the Colony in a ragged and destitute condition.

15. In this building I saw also a number of Poor Law cases, that is men sent to Hadleigh by Boards of Guardians. The overseers informed me that many of them were respectable hard-working men and that, although London bred, in most cases they were working well.

16. Afterwards I visited the lowest grade dormitory, where men are put when first they come to the Colony. The bedding here is not so good as that in the higher class, but it consists of a seaweed mattress, covered in American cloth, with eight military blankets and a pillow to each bed. There are twenty beds in a division, and by each of them stands a box provided for the storage of the belongings of its occupant. Also there are admirable regulations to ensure cleanliness and comfort, and at the end of the building is the cubicle in which an orderly sleeps. Smoking is prohibited in the bedchambers, and theft, I was assured, is exceedingly rare.

17. In the higher grade dormitory, which I saw also, the bedding is superior, and the sleeping places are divided into ten bed compartments. A man is raised in his grade if he works well and satisfactorily and his general character and conduct are proved to be good. If he is raised to this higher class dormitory he is also raised to a higher class dietary, and receives food of rather better quality and more ample in quantity.

18. Here I may state that the men are, as far as possible, paid by piece work, and there have been some in the colony who have taken as much as fifteen shillings per week, in addition to their board and lodging. At the time of my visit one man was receiving nine shillings a week for clay digging, and another, working on the market garden, seven

9 *

shillings and threepence per week, in either case plus their
board and lodging. Both of these men came from a London Poor Law Union. The average man, however, is paid
about three shillings per week, of course in addition to board
and lodging.

19. Next I visited the laundry, where all the washing is
done by men. The colonists parcel up their clothes and
place them on their beds in bundles. These are collected,
washed by the laundrymen, who are also colonists, and returned to the bed free of charge on the Saturday morning.
Those men are employed in washing who prove not strong
enough to work outside in all weathers.

20. Attached to this building are four bathrooms, which
upon four nights a week any man can use.

I give specimen conversations with a man named Dorey
and a lad named Barnes, whom I saw here.

Dorey.

Q. How long have you been here?
A. Four and a half years, sir.
Q. What were you before you came?
A. Sanitary engineer.
Q. Went astray, I suppose?
A. Yes.
Q. Not astray now? Doing all right?
A. Yes.
Q. You are superintendent of the laundry?
A. Yes.

Barnes.

Q. Where do you come from?
A. London, sir.
Q. What were you doing there?
A. Only walking about the streets.
Q. Why were you walking about the streets? Have you
a mother?
A. Yes.
Q. Could not your mother support you?
A. No.
Q. You were getting a living the best way you could,

and then the Salvation Army found you and you were sent
to this colony by a lady ?

A. Yes.

Q. How long have you been here now ?

A. Four months, sir.

21. I then went on to the hospital, but there was no one
in it except the orderly. It seemed a very suitable building which is attended by a medical practitioner from Leigh
every day, who is paid a fixed salary. Beyond it was a
dormitory of forty beds occupied by some of the London
unemployed.

22. I also saw the brickyards which do not need especial
description. They are very fine places of the sort, and turn
out enormous quantities of bricks. One of them has a
chimney stack 150 feet high, built of the Colony bricks
and for the most part by Colony labour. This yard is
actuated by a steam engine of 350 brake horse-power which
cost £800. When the new machine which was being put
in is completed, it will turn out 6,000 bricks a day, and if
it proves successful others will be added.

There are several of these brickworks, and in one of them
we saw hand-moulded bricks being made which fetch as
much as eighty shillings per 1,000. The office clerk of this
yard, I was informed, once was a major in the British Army,
and all the men employed there had been redeemed upon
the Colony.

23. Further, I inspected the Colony agriculture. The poultry farm, where prize birds are bred, was very interesting,
although, owing to the character of the seasons, it has not
paid during the last two years. The great difficulty with
which the manager of this poultry farm has to contend is
the damp clay soil, that in spite of every care and protection
kills a number of chickens in very cold weather, especially
those of what are called the "lighter" varieties. Indeed
for this reason Brahmas, Dorkings, Minorcas and some
other fowls which love a light gravel soil will not do here.
White Wyandottes, Partridge Wyandottes, Orpingtons, white
and barred Rocks and many others flourish however, and
some pens of five birds have been sold recently at as high
as £7 per pen.

In all, 2,500 head of stock birds are kept, which are looked

after by an expert superintendent, who has been in charge
for ten years, and one underman, the remaining labour
being done by the colonists. Hearson's 100-egg incubators
are used, but the foster mothers are made by the colonists
themselves.

There is also a splendid herd of pedigree middle-white
sows. At the time of my visit there were 250 pigs upon
the Colony, but in summer the number sometimes rises to
500. They are kept in an excellent range of sties, which
are well ventilated, with proper sloping floors and outside
yards.

24. Close to the sties is a field of good land measuring
about 15 acres, which last season yielded a record crop of
potatoes, while from the next field in the same year came
swedes that took the third prize at the Dairy Show at the
Agricultural Hall in London.

Near by stands a line of ten cottages, good substantial
buildings in red brick, with gable windows. These cottages
cost a total of £2,000, and are let at a rental of six shillings
per week, inclusive of water rate, to gangers and others
employed by the Salvation Army.

25. Adjoining the cottages is a range of glasshouses run
by the market garden department. The first of these was
full of mint, almost ready to cut for the London market.
Next came one with garden stuff, such as chrysanthemum
and geranium cuttings and some foliage plants; then another
of mint, a paying winter crop, which was shortly to be sup-
planted by tomatoes, that stood ready in pots in another
house. Beneath the stages of these houses rhubarb is
forced. At the time of my visit it was being pulled and
done up in bundles to be marketed at Southend, where it
fetches one shilling and threepence per dozen bundles.
Also there were cold frames planted with lettuce, and behind them a rose bed.

26. Further, I visited the dairy where the milk of nineteen
cows is dealt with, also I saw the cows themselves and the
bull, a very fine red Lincoln. This dairy is well fitted with
milk coolers, and Alfa Lavel separator, churns and steam
cleansing plant. Near by are the excellent stabling for
twelve horses and a number of boxes for cows and fatting
beasts.

27. Opposite these buildings lie the Colony allotments, which can be taken by the colonists free of charge, all the produce being their own property. Each plot measures about six rods.

28. Further, I inspected the Salvation Army School, where I found about 100 boys and girls singing a hymn, some 60 per cent. of these children coming from Hadleigh village. The Salvationist schoolmaster, Mr. Collins, is a properly qualified man, and the school receives a county grant.

Mr. Collins put various questions to the scholars upon religious, mathematical and general knowledge subjects, all of which they answered intelligently in my presence.

29. Near to the school is the citadel, or gathering hall, a large corrugated iron building with seats for about 400 persons. Here religious services are held, and every Saturday night a popular concert. At these gatherings every colonist is expected to attend, the object of them being to provide entertainment which will induce men to keep away from the public-house.

30. I may mention here that I was informed that the relationship existing between the Army officials and other religious bodies in the neighbourhood is good. It is said that no pressure is brought to bear upon any man to force him to conform to the religious principles of the Army. In proof of this it was reported to me that on the Sunday previous to my visit the manager, Mr. Iliffe, had attended the Parish Church, accompanied by about 100 of the colonists.

31. Lastly I was shown the Inebriates' Home, an old mansion with a large garden, which has been adapted to this purpose, and is licensed for twenty male inebriates. One of the rooms was filled with wood carvings that had been executed by the patients and were for sale. Inebriates are taken in here at a charge of from twenty-five to thirty shillings per week, and the Salvation Army Authorities stated to me that from 60 to 70 per cent. of them are permanently reclaimed after an average period of eight months' treatment.

32. I forgot to mention that near to the residence of the manager is a large store. Here vegetables, etc., are brought, sorted, loaded into vans and sent to Southend, where the Colony has its own market, in which the produce is sold at wholesale rates to various dealers.

33. To sum up, the Hadleigh Settlement is to my mind an instance of the extraordinary results which can be attained by wretched men working on land that the ordinary agriculturist would also call wretched. Putting aside its most valuable charitable and social uses, it shows what could be done with much cold English soil if only sufficient capital and labour were applied to that soil.

34. General Booth and other of the Army Authorities, however, informed me that they had been much hampered in their efforts to house and provide work for yet larger numbers of destitute persons at Hadleigh by the action of the Rural District Authorities, who insist upon the carrying out of regulations as to methods of building and the material used, which the Salvation Army managers, as practical persons, consider to be absurd, vexatious, and needlessly expensive.

35. It is a remarkable fact that there are no policemen on duty on the Hadleigh Colony, as, notwithstanding the rough nature of many of its inhabitants, they are not needed there. Indeed, three years have passed since a drunk and disorderly case against any colonist was brought before the Magistrates. This immunity from crime doubtless arises from the kind but strict discipline practised in the Colony, the moral tone which has grown up there, and from the circumstance that temperance is enforced.

If by chance a man is found to be drunk he is warned, and should he repeat his offence he is sent off the place. There is practically no need for any other form of punishment.

H. RIDER HAGGARD,
Commissioner.

No. 34.

REMARKS ON THE WORK OF THE VACANT LOTS CULTIVATION ASSOCIATION AT PHILADELPHIA, UNITED STATES OF AMERICA.

On the 6th of March, 1905, I attended a meeting at the house of Mr. Kirkbride at Philadelphia, where Mr. Powell, the Manager of the Vacant Lots Association, who had accompanied me from New York, gave a very interesting lecture, illustrated by views, on the work of the Association.

Briefly, the history of this Philadelphia Association is as follows: Eight or nine years ago, it occurred to certain charitable people in Philadelphia, that some of the large quantity of land in and around the city which has been purchased and is reserved for building sites, might be put to a profitable temporary use if permission could be gotten for poor folk to cultivate it in summer.

There seems to have been considerable difficulty, however, in obtaining such permission. Out of a total of many thousand acres—I gathered that in all the unoccupied area, indeed, amounts to between 20,000 and 30,000 acres—only 300 acres have been so loaned by their owners, and these are held subject to a ten days' notice to quit. The lecturer stated that were it possible to obtain it, a very large extra quantity of land could be thus employed, as the demand for gardens is great and increasing. Meanwhile such gardens as are cultivated have proved a wonderful success.

I believe I am right in saying that whereas the total charitable expenditure upon them amounts up to date to about £6,000, the total value of the produce sold of them up to date by their cultivators amounts to about £60,000.

The moral and physical results upon those members of the population to whom the gardens have been allotted, including those gardens which are given to school children to handle, are very remarkable. Men who were drunkards have ceased to drink ; men and women who were in extreme poverty have managed, by their help, to eke out a comfortable existence, and men who were very weak and feeble

have become strong.   Moreover, another result has been a
curious heightening of the moral tone, both of the cultivators
of the plots and of members of the class from which they
spring.   Thus, although these allotments are practically un-
protected, theft of the fruits and vegetables grown upon
them is, in fact, unknown.

In all these and other ways it would seem, therefore, that
so far the working of the plan has proved practicable, profitable, and advantageous to those whom it was desired to aid.

A further fruit of it is that a number of persons have obtained a practical knowledge of the art of cultivation, which
knowledge I believe some of them have put to use in a
wider field.   It must be borne in mind, however, that these
ends could not have been reached except through the aid of
charity.   The land is given for nothing; it is manured for
nothing, with refuse from the city, or with artificial dressings
provided by the Association.   Seeds are also given for nothing, the labourer being expected to furnish only his own
tools.

On the following day I drove to visit the Vacant Lots.
Passing through three or four miles of the city we came, at
length, to land not yet built upon.   There, upon each side of
the roadway, lay some of the lots enclosed respectively by a
low and broken stone wall, and with an iron fence in which
were intertwined branches of trees.

Of course, at this time of the year, with snow about and
actually falling, there was not much to be seen upon the
ground itself, although the evidences of the labour of the
lot-holders were plentiful in the shape of the dry stems of
Indian corn and old bean stalks.

I observed also that upon some of the lots the gardeners
had themselves collected piles of manure, to be used as soon
as the frost was out of the ground, which I should add is a
clay-loam on clay.   On others were "hales" or pits, containing cabbages, carrots, parsnips, beets, etc., grown upon
the land last summer, and stored here until they can be
profitably disposed of or used.   Also rough sheds had been
erected to contain tools and afford shelter to the workers.

Passing on I came to another tract of land situated between
railway lines, which for three years was cultivated under the
auspices of the Vacant Lots Association, but at the end of

that period had been taken away from them because there was some prospect of its being sold. The owners, however, allowed the gardeners to continue to work their lots, which five families are still doing, without any assistance in money or kind from the Association. This instance is of interest, since it shows how, when once the desire to hold and to work land has been established, it will gratify itself even in the face of difficulties and of a lack of outside support.

Near by to this land I saw cottages which are inhabited by some of the poor of this district, whereof it would be difficult to say more than that they stand among trees, and, therefore, have the advantage of the country air. In appearance, however, they were certainly somewhat wretched looking when compared with most of the dwellings of a similar sort in England. For instance, one of them was built of boarding painted red, with shabby out-houses and having its sanitary conveniences open to the road. Others were more substantially constructed of stone, washed with concrete, having wooden roofs covered with slag.

These dwellings contained four rooms, two below and two above, and I daresay are warmer and more comfortable than their outward appearance would seem to suggest. The prevailing note about them, and one which, speaking generally, is not very common in country cottages in England, was the strange untidiness of their surroundings. The palings were broken down, irregular and unmended, while in the surrounding plots, where a garden should have been, lay heaps of rubbish.

I was informed that the tenants of these shanties earn from £1 to 30s. per week, plus any extra money which may be brought in by their children who work in the mills close at hand. For their poor dwellings they pay a rent of from twenty to thirty shillings a month.

It seemed to me that the weak point about this Vacant Lots Association is that it is a charity pure and simple, unanimated by any life of its own, and, therefore, sooner or later, when the subscriptions fail, or, for some cause unforeseen, interest in it flags, liable to die. Indeed, in at least two other American cities which I visited, this has happened. Meanwhile it does much good work, not the least part of which is that it teaches to indigent townsfolk the uses of the land, and shows them what profit and health can be earned out of that land. If, after a while, a rent were charged for these plots it would put matters on a better basis. This, however, is difficult where very poor folk are concerned, where also they are liable to be called upon to give up their holdings at ten days' notice.

H. RIDER HAGGARD,
Commissioner.

COLONIST'S HOUSE, FORT ROMIE.

COLONIST'S HOUSE, FORT ROMIE.

No. 35.

APPROXIMATE STATEMENT SHOWING ESTIMATED COST IN POUNDS STERLING OF SETTLING COLONISTS IN CANADA (EXCLUSIVE OF LAND).

Savings from one column can be transferred to another according to relative cost of Transportation, Lumber, Live-stock, etc.

Families.	Souls.	Acres of Land.	1. Cottages and Barns.	2. Live-stock.	3. Implements and Fencing.	4. Five months' food or allowance.	5. Seed and feed.	6. Transport.	Total.	Yearly Repayments by Colonists on New Zealand plan of 6 per cent, (including 1 per cent, Sinking Fund).
			£ 70	£ 30	£ 20	£ 20	£ 20	£ 40	£ 200	£ 12
1	5	160	70	30	20	20	20	40	200	12
100	500	16,000	7,000	3,000	2,000	2,000	2,000	4,000	20,000	1,200
500	2,500	80,000	35,000	15,000	10,000	10,000	10,000	20,000	100,000	6,000
1,000	5,000	160,000	70,000	30,000	20,000	20,000	20,000	40,000	200,000	12,000
1,500	7,500	240,000	105,000	45,000	30,000	30,000	30,000	60,000	300,000	18,000
2,000	10,000	320,000	140,000	60,000	40,000	40,000	40,000	80,000	400,000	24,000
5,000	25,000	800,000	350,000	150,000	100,000	100,000	100,000	200,000	1,000,000	60,000
10,000	50,000	1,600,000	700,000	300,000	200,000	200,000	200,000	400,000	2,000,000	120,000
25,000	125,000	4,000,000	1,750,000	750,000	500,000	500,000	500,000	1,000,000	5,000,000	300,000
50,000	250,000	8,000,000	3,500,000	1,500,000	1,000,000	1,000,000	1,000,000	2,000,000	10,000,000	600,000

It would probably be advisable to furnish the Colonists with materials and live-stock, making the purchases for them in bulk.
Columns 3, 4 and 5 could perhaps be managed through Village Banks of the Raffeisen type.
Although the land is given free by the Canadian Government, I suggest that a small charge should be made to the Settler of say from 6s. to 12s. per acre, to form the nucleus of a Colonisation Fund, etc.
This Transportation Estimate is somewhat uncertain; it would depend on the location of the land, and cost of reaching it from the seaboard.

No. 36.

APPROXIMATE STATEMENT SHOWING ANNUAL CHARGES, INCOME, AND PROBABLE SURPLUS OF SUGGESTED CANADIAN COLONISATION SCHEME.

Families.	Souls.	Acres of Land.	Loan for Settlement (Land free).	Annual Charges.					Annual Income.			Total Surplus available for Colonisation Fund.
				Interest on Loan at 3 per cent.	Sinking Fund, 1 per cent.	Management and General Improvements, 1 per cent.	Failures, Sundries, and Bad Debts, ½ per cent.	Total.	Interest and Sinking Fund from Settlers on loan, 6 per cent.	Instalment on land at 12s. per acre, payable 32 years.	Total.	
			£	£	£	£	£	£	£	£	£	£
1	5	160	200	6	2	2	1	11	12	3	15	4
100	500	16,000	20,000	600	200	200	100	1,100	1,200	300	1,500	400
1,000	5,000	160,000	200,000	6,000	2,000	2,000	1,000	11,000	12,000	3,000	15,000	4,000
1,500	7,500	240,000	300,000	9,000	3,000	3,000	1,500	16,500	18,000	4,500	22,500	6,000
2,000	10,000	320,000	400,000	12,000	4,000	4,000	2,000	22,000	24,000	6,000	30,000	8,000
5,000	25,000	800,000	1,000,000	30,000	10,000	10,000	5,000	55,000	60,000	15,000	75,000	20,000
10,000	50,000	1,600,000	2,000,000	60,000	20,000	20,000	10,000	110,000	120,000	30,000	150,000	40,000
25,000	125,000	4,000,000	5,000,000	150,000	50,000	50,000	25,000	275,000	300,000	75,000	375,000	100,000
50,000	250,000	8,000,000	10,000,000	300,000	100,000	100,000	50,000	550,000	600,000	150,000	750,000	200,000

No. 37.

APPROXIMATE STATEMENT SHOWING SECURITY FOR LOAN TO CARRY OUT SUGGESTED SCHEME OF CANADIAN COLONISATION.

Families.	Souls.	Acres of Land.	Loan.	Present value of unoccupied land at £1 per acre.	Security for Loan.		Total.	Value of land in say 10 years when the rest is colonised at £5 per acre.[1]
					Value of land when occupied at £2 per acre.	Value of Buildings at cost of materials.		
1	5	160	£ 200	£ 160	£ 320	£ 70	£ 390	£ 800
100	500	16,000	20,000	16,000	32,000	7,000	39,000	80,000
1,000	5,000	160,000	200,000	160,000	320,000	70,000	390,000	800,000
1,500	7,500	240,000	300,000	240,000	480,000	105,000	585,000	1,200,000
2,000	10,000	320,000	400,000	320,000	640,000	140,000	780,000	1,600,000
5,000	25,000	800,000	1,000,000	800,000	1,600,000	350,000	1,950,000	4,000,000
10,000	50,000	1,600,000	2,000,000	1,600,000	3,200,000	700,000	3,900,000	8,000,000
50,000	250,000	8,000,000	10,000,000	8,000,000	16,000,000	3,500,000	19,500,000	40,000,000

[1] This allows nothing for implements, live-stock, and general improvements.

No. 38.

Telegram from His Excellency Earl Grey, Governor-General
of Canada, to Commissioner H. Rider Haggard.

To Rider Haggard, New York.

19th April, 1905.

Pleasant voyage to you all.   May the Report you take
home weave Canada closer than ever into one piece with
England and be the means of providing happy homes for
thousands of the worthy disinherited who, without hope,
throng the city life of Great Britain.

GREY.

SOME PRESS OPINIONS ON THE FOREGOING REPORT AND SCHEME OF NATIONAL LAND SETTLEMENT.

The Times (Leading article).—Mr. Rider Haggard has completed with commendable despatch a work of great interest to all who have at heart the national welfare. . . . On the whole, Mr. Rider Haggard brings back a distinctly favourable account of the experiments in America. He records some failures or miscalculations ; he records still more impressive successes; and he presents the outlines of a scheme, framed with the lessons of the American Agricultural Colonies before him, and after consultation with men of practical experience, for colonisation on a large scale. With the object which he had in view there will be general sympathy. The drift to the town; the severance from the land of people who become degraded physically and otherwise in great cities ; the sight of vast tracks of fertile land lying uncultivated, while thousands annually move helplessly and blindly towards cities, there to mix in a population of waifs and drift-wood ; the "tendency to race-ruin, a product of our Western culture," due greatly to living in crowded quarters of great cities—all that is so grave an evil that any alleviation of it is to be prized. . . . Mr. Rider Haggard has done a public service in collecting the information contained in his Report, and in making suggestions which may prove fruitful. . . . Mr. Rider Haggard will, it is to be hoped, be enabled to continue his inquiries, and tell us how his plan can be carried out in England, dear land, excessive rates and the rising demands of rural district Councils notwithstanding.

The Standard (London).—The country is to be congratulated upon the obviously thorough and energetic manner in which Mr. Haggard has performed the task imposed upon him. The subject of this very valuable document is one in which the public . . . will take a lively interest. Particularly should we welcome a scheme for the emigration of those classes of the community which are cared for in The Salvation Army Colonies, and with which Mr. Haggard is specially concerned. . . . We may fairly hazard the hope that the project will survive in its main features any criticism to which it may be subjected.

Morning Post.—The whole scheme (*i.e.* the Unemployed Workmen Bill) appears to us to proceed on wrong lines. In the profoundly interesting Report by Mr. Rider Haggard which was published yesterday . . . a wiser and far more hopeful policy is advocated. . . . We urge . . . the fullest consideration for such plans and extreme caution in dealing with the problem in the manner proposed by the Government.

10 145

Daily Telegraph.—His conclusions are confidently affirmative, and the Report now published as a Blue Book, in which he frames the plan which he thinks would prove most conducive to the desired end, will possibly remain at the same time the most important and the least read of his varied literary achievements.

Daily News.—The importance of such a mission can hardly be over-estimated, in view of its bearing on the unemployed question here, and Mr. Rider Haggard has carried it through so thoroughly and practically that the result is a Report of the first importance. . . . We hope that Mr. Haggard's Report will be widely read, not merely in summaries, but also in its original fulness.

Daily Chronicle.—Mr. Rider Haggard's Report is, as we anticipated some weeks ago, a most interesting and suggestive document; and, as we shall see, it is by no means only in the air. The Salvation Army and the Rhodes Trustees are to be congratulated on having been the means of procuring so valuable a collection of data for what may become a great Imperial experiment. . . . Mr. Lyttelton selected Mr. Rider Haggard for the work; he could hardly have made a better choice; . . . Mr. Rider Haggard finds the touch of magic in "turning to practical account the public credit and the waste forces of benevolence ".

Daily Mail.—The Report . . . is full of interest.

The Daily Express.—For all who are attempting, in whatever capacity, to grapple with the problem of providing an outlet for the population of our overcrowded cities, a vista of hope and encouragement is opened by Mr. Haggard's Report on The Salvation Army Over-Sea Colonies. . . . For so excellent an end the Imperial Government should have no difficulty in devising financial means.

. . . .

Mr. Rider Haggard's plan for settling the landless men of the English towns on the manless lands of Canada has aroused general interest. It is welcomed alike by Commissioner Booth Tucker, of The Salvation Army, who founded the Farm Colonies in the United States, which Mr. Haggard takes as models for his scheme, and by Mr. W. T. R. Preston, the Canadian Commissioner for Emigration in London, who has done so much in the last few years to direct the stream of emigration to Canada.

"It is an Imperial scheme," said Mr. Preston to a *Gazette and Express* representative yesterday. "It relieves England of thousands of families who have no outlook here, and who will probably cost the ratepayers much money to maintain. The enormous advantage which this surplus population would be to Canada, or to other British Colonies, can hardly be estimated by people at home.

"Canada ought to get 250,000 emigrants a year to develop her lands. Last year we got 134,000, of whom rather more than a third came from England, the rest from the Continent and the United States.

"We would rather have more people from Great Britain, and this scheme for settling British people in Canada is a real piece of Imperial consolidation."

The Globe.—While very varying opinions will obtain as to the practicability of Mr. Rider Haggard's scheme for checking the continuous drifting of rural labour to towns, there can be no dissent from warm approval of the patriotism directing his endeavours.

The Evening Standard and St. James's Gazette.—Mr. Rider Haggard's Blue Book published this week may be the beginning of a new movement to fill up the waste lands of the Empire with men and women, and boys and girls, whose "limbs were made in England". At least it ought to lead to such a result, for it suggests a plan which seems practicable and sound, and only needs wise prevision and concerted effort to be successful.

The Echo.—Mr. Rider Haggard's extremely interesting Report on the possibility of encouraging emigration from the slums to the Colonies is certain of a favourable reception. . . . That something must be done to turn back the tide which carries the rural population to our towns we are all agreed. . . . At least it is clear from Mr. Haggard's Report that the trial is worth making. There ought to be no hesitation about providing the necessary funds.

Pall Mall Gazette.—Mr. Rider Haggard has found success realised in those agricultural settlements which have been used for the absorption of some sections of the lapsed masses from American cities, and he is encouraged to believe that a similar effort to dispose of a portion of our own derelict population in Canada would afford a partial cure for social problems. The Canadian Government is prepared to be liberal in the matter of land, and The Salvation Army would no doubt place its organisation at our disposal as in the case of the American undertakings. If emigration from this country is to continue, it could not take a better form than that of transmuting those who are an economic failure at home into prosporous and useful citizens of another province of the Empire. It is a project, of course, which cannot be executed without public assistance, and those who are prepared to undertake it must be ready to discount a certain element of failure and disappointment until the lines of safe development have been discovered and established.

The Daily Mirror.—The great thing is to get it started, and to realise that we are "laying great bases" for the future . . . and the sooner we begin the better, for the Problem of the Poor grows more pressing every day.

The Morning Advertiser.—His scheme is thoroughly practical and sympathetic. He believes, and seems to have good grounds for the belief, that it would work well, and to the great advantage of the Empire and the race. . . . His scheme is certainly deserving of the most attentive consideration, and indeed it is easy to be convinced that it deserves immediate trial.

The Spectator.—Mr. Rider Haggard has issued a Report which is both a valuable account of an interesting and successful experiment, and an indication of a possible solution for some of our unemployed problems. . . . The scheme has obvious difficulties, but it is at any rate a suggestion which is well worth the most serious consideration.

10 *

The Saturday Review.—Mr. Rider Haggard's Report on The Salvation Army Colonies in the United States and Hadleigh is, as Mr. Gerald Balfour described in the debate on the Unemployed Bill, hopeful. . . . There will, no doubt, be the usual outcry about the perils of State interference ; but Mr. Haggard believes in the vital necessity of settling people on the land, and is convinced that this can only be done satisfactorily by the State. Whenever a man looks at facts as they are, the "self-help" apostle appears foolish.

The People.—All I can say is, I hope and trust the Scheme will be taken up at once, and that we in this country shall not lag behind the vigorous efforts that Canada is ready and waiting to make to help us in this direction.

Reynolds's Weekly Newspaper.—The Official Report by Mr. Rider Haggard on The Salvation Army Land Settlements in the United States is a valuable contribution to the solution of the problem of the decentralisation of the population. The publication of this Report on the eve of the passing of the second reading of the Unemployed Bill in the House of Commons by a huge majority has a special significance.

To-Day.—Though there are one or two things in Mr. Rider Haggard's Report on the possibilities of Canadian immigration with which I am not in complete sympathy, I fully agree with him in his suggestion that something might be done to colonise England on the same lines as the proposed Canadian settlements.

The Outlook.—There is much instructive matter in Mr. Rider Haggard's Blue Book, which contains a critical account of The Salvation Army Colonies in the United States and Canada.

The Mark Lane Express.—Home Colonies of this kind might prove to be something more than refuges for the man who has been unfortunate in the town, but who still has brain and muscle, and is possessed by the desire to work out an honourable destiny. Such Colonies as these might prove labour nurseries—nurseries of that labour whose absence from the land is precipitating danger and menace. . . . This Report of Mr. Rider Haggard's, with its clear-eyed prescience, and its generous pulsations of sympathy, and its statesmanlike grasp. . . .

The Guardian.—A "Commission of one" as a means of investigation is likely to grow in favour with the public from the prompt and businesslike way in which Mr. Rider Haggard has despatched the work which the Colonial Office gave him to do. . . . Mr. Haggard finds that the Salvation Army has made mistakes, as was to be expected ; it has also profited by them; and generally can point to a measure of success quite compensating for previous failures.

The Christian.—At last we have a really practical scheme for dealing with the question of overcrowding. The Report of Mr. Rider Haggard, as Special Commissioner, to inquire into the working of The Salvation Army's Land Scheme in the United States, is enthusiastically in favour of this Scheme being applied imperially. In the States prairie land has been converted into arable land, worked by men who a short time ago were stifling in large cities. The whole Report should be read in order to gain an idea of the benefit this scheme has been. Now the Canadian Government offers a free grant of 240,000 acres for a similar purpose, and the land is offered to English workers. Such redistribution of land and workers is the only way out of the difficulty of overcrowding. The centres must be thinned in favour of the solitary places.

Country Life.—Mr. Rider Haggard's Report on The Salvation Army Colonies in the United States is a document of the utmost importance to all who have the welfare of the country at heart. . . . There is, however, a residue who would gladly escape from the sordid struggle of the towns, and it is for their benefit that Mr. Rider Haggard has outlined a scheme which we hope will find favour with the English people and their Government as it has already received acceptance from President Roosevelt in the United States and from Sir Wilfrid Laurier.

South Africa.—The basis of a thoroughly practical scheme by means of which the manless land and the landless man will be brought into association, and we look forward with every confidence to seeing it put into operation in Rhodesia and other South African Colonies at no distant date.

A comprehensive scheme carried out on the lines indicated by Messrs. Booth-Tucker and Haggard would, we are convinced, be a financial success from the very beginning, and there is no reason why immediate steps should not be taken to put it into effect.

The African World.—Mr. Rider Haggard's Report on The Salvation Army Colonies in Canada is an eminently practical document, and should lead to definite action on the part of the Government . . . he advises the Imperial Government to send a special Commissioner to South Africa to see what arrangements can be made there for receiving immigrants from this country. Writing from both personal knowledge and on the evidence of experts, Mr. Haggard regards South Africa, and particularly Rhodesia, as well suited for the carrying out of land settlement projects. . . . The need for white settlers in the vast territory south of the Zambesi is overwhelming, and any well-considered scheme backed up by the Imperial authorities would almost certainly command the support of every South African Government. Careful investigation and thoughtful outlining of the plan to be followed are indispensable preliminaries.

The Review of Reviews.—What more need is there to labour the point? The scheme is business-like, sound and ready. The agents are waiting.

The World's Work and Play.—Though Mr. Rider Haggard's enthusiasm in advocating his plan is not concealed, his ardour has not blinded him to facts, which are set forth with precision and in minute detail.

The Friend.—The overcrowded condition of certain districts in our large cities affords further evidence of the need of some national effort for the relief of the congestion. Towards such an end H. Rider Haggard's able Report issued last week as a Government Blue Book is an illuminating contribution. . . . The Report is one deserving the careful thought and study of social reformers.

The Sanitary Record.—The scheme of land settlement promulgated by Mr. Rider Haggard in his Report to the Colonial Office is bold and interesting. . . .
The question will have to be considered from the point of view of the national interests as a whole—in a large and sympathetic spirit, no doubt, but at the same time with prudence and caution.

The Manchester Guardian.—Mr. Rider Haggard's Report should command the earnest attention of every one who has at heart the relief of the congestion of our cities. A better choice could hardly have been made ; Mr. Haggard is not only a skilled agriculturist, but a man whose heart has been profoundly stirred by the depopulation of our rural districts and the corresponding congestion of our cities.

Manchester Evening News.—There is true statesmanship in this new scheme, not the least striking and attractive features of it being the method of securing peasant-proprietorship on terms which defend the settler's independence and freedom, and protect also the money invested by the State or the municipality for its initiation and working. It means a great reform, which once begun in the Colonies will have to be started in the Mother Country.

Manchester Evening Chronicle.—Mr. Rider Haggard's Report on over-sea settlements is a hopeful sign of the times. There is a wide agreement that if the congestion of the cities is to be remedied and its evils abolished, something more than the symptoms will have to be treated. . . . We echo his hope that there may follow a separate memorandum on the possibility of similar colonies at home.

The Yorkshire Daily Post.—The Report issued by Mr. Rider Haggard upon The Salvation Army Colonies in the United States and the possibility of relieving the pressure of the "submerged" classes upon civilisation in this country, is of great interest. . . . Mr. Rider Haggard rightly praises Canada for offering lands free for settlements to be made through the agency of The Salvation Army ; it is the high-water mark so far of Canada's Imperial institutions. The work of The Salvation Army in this direction might well be encouraged, within prudent limitations ; those who object to national funds being applied in this manner may be reminded that to reduce the congestion in this country is to lessen a fertile source of high poor-rates.

The Yorkshire Herald.—It is evident that there is a very distinct trend of opinion in favour of work on lines such as Mr. Rider Haggard and Mr. Booth Tucker have sketched out, and we trust that there may be careful public and Governmental consideration of a matter promising so well for the national weal.
Mr. Rider Haggard's Report . . . is a document of exceptional interest and importance. It confirms in a marked degree the wisdom of the suggestion made by the Rhodes Trustees that a Commissioner should be appointed to make diligent and impartial inquiry into the subject, and it leaves no doubt that Mr. Lyttelton's selection of Mr.

Haggard for the work was the outcome of a keen appreciation alike of the possibilities and gravity of the mission and of the peculiar fitness of the man whom he asked to undertake the duty. . . . A Report which will have the greatest value for all who are earnestly seeking a solution of some very vital problems in our national life. . . . The keynote of Mr. Haggard's proposal is business success, as well as national welfare.

The Yorkshire Evening News.—Mr. Haggard's visit to The Salvation Army Settlements in the United States has been fruitful of suggestion, and the Report will be read with wide interest. . . . The material the Report provides for the better study of the unemployed question must be accepted with satisfaction. . . . The result particularly gratifying. . . . When city labour does adapt itself to agricultural purposes, the keener instincts developed in the towns are found to be of immense advantage.

Birmingham Gazette.— . . . It is to be hoped that we in this country shall not lag behind the vigorous efforts which Canada is ready and willing to make.

Birmingham Evening Despatch.—Mr. Rider Haggard's Report upon his mission to The Salvation Army Settlements in the United States, and the feasibility of establishing a similar scheme within the British Empire is full of interesting possibilities for the solution of one of the most bitter problems of the day.

Birmingham Post.—Mr. Rider Haggard . . . has presented his Report and it has just been issued as a Blue Book. Its appearance is timely. . . . The Government must be prepared to advance sufficient money to work the scheme satisfactorily from the first, or rather to guarantee interest on the capital required. But if the Government is prepared to do this to start land settlements in the Colonies, why should it not make more liberal advances to those who would gladly become small-holders at home? The Report is full of interesting matter, and will well repay careful reading.

The Sheffield Independent.—A document that is bound to be studied with keen attention by all who are interested in the important branch of social reform, the purpose of which is summed up in the words, " Back to the land ". . . . By his knowledge of the economics of agriculture, and his attentive study of the problems connected with the land, he has fully qualified himself for the inquiry which the Colonial Office invited him to undertake—the inquiry the results of which are before us. . . . A Report that reaches such conclusions is one that deserves and will assuredly obtain sympathetic consideration from every social reformer.

The Sheffield Daily Telegraph.—Experience has shown it is possible successfully to transplant indigent people of the labouring class from towns to the land. . . . We gather that Mr. Haggard is strongly in favour of making use of The Salvation Army Organisation in the selection of suitable persons, and, in fact, in running the settlements, and his suggestion of a working arrangement of this kind, if the system ever does occupy public attention as a State business, appears to be worthy of consideration.

East Anglian Daily Times.—Mr. Rider Haggard's Report . . . is, on the whole, an encouraging document and leads to the belief that in these Labour Colonies does in part lie the solution of the problem of the unemployed. . . . The net result of the experiments is to show that indigent people of the agricultural labourer class can be settled upon the land and there do well, and that such persons can even be taken from towns and prosper. . . . All the data, furnished by a competent and sympathetic observer, can now be considered and judged, and a very important contribution to the solution of the problem is furnished for all social reformers to consider. . . . Mr. Rider Haggard did the work which he was commissioned to do in America with characteristic thoroughness. His report on The Salvation Army Colonies abroad is a mine of useful information. It is certainly to be hoped that it will be turned to a useful purpose.

Eastern Daily Press.—Mr. Rider Haggard's Report upon his American tour and his inspection of The Salvation Army Colonies there . . . is a document of exceeding interest. He reports strongly in favour of the attempt to relieve the overcrowding of our cities with destitute persons by the establishment of agricultural colonies. Given certain conditions, he is convinced of the possible success of such a scheme.

Essex County Chronicle.—Putting aside its most valuable, charitable, and social uses, it shows what could be done with much cold English soil if only sufficient capital and labour were applied to that soil.

Midland Evening News.—Mr. Rider Haggard's Report on The Salvation Army Settlements in the United States is a valuable contribution to the discussion of the problem of how to get the destitute poor back to the land. He shows with remarkable clearness that the success or failure of such experiments depends essentially on the class of men selected for the settlements.

The Lancashire Daily Post.—Mr. Rider Haggard's Report on his investigations into the question of colonising settlements for the unemployed offers, on the whole, the best practical solution we have seen yet of this grave problem.

With the offer by Canada of ten townships for the experiment, there seems no reason why a scheme should not be developed and promptly put in hand.

Liverpool Daily Courier.—But the unemployed question cannot be shirked. . . . A fillip has been given to the discussion of the " back to the land " idea by the publication of Mr. Rider Haggard's Report upon the experiments of The Salvation Army in the United States. . . . The subject is, therefore, one that requires the most earnest thought of statesmen, for the state of things in the cities is increasingly ominous.

The Lancaster Guardian.—Mr. Rider Haggard's Report to the Colonial Office on the Farm Settlements of The Salvation Army in North America should command the earnest attention of every one who has at heart the relief of the congestion of our cities. The contrast from the squalid slum-room to the cosy cottages of the Farm Colony is remarkable.

The Leicester Daily Post.—Mr. Rider Haggard's Report is a most important document, and the conclusions and recommendations which Mr. Haggard set forth demand serious attention. The praise he bestowed upon the Work of The Salvation Army in this direction upon his return from the States again finds expression in his Report, and he pays them a higher compliment still in the matter of their Organisation. Mr. Haggard insists upon the necessity of a judicious selection of men in the first instance ; and here it is that he bears testimony to the value of the work of The Salvation Army. It would be impossible, he says, for this selection to be made by any officials appointed for the purpose. In his opinion a body like The Army alone could do this work, and this work they are both able and willing to undertake. We should be inclined to supplement The Army's services, however, by those of such bodies as our own Citizen's Aid Society. But that is a detail. What we are most concerned about is the putting into practice of Mr. Haggard's suggestions, believing that by their adoption a great step forward would be taken towards the settlement of the unemployed problem.

The Nottingham Daily Express.—The Report . . . will repay careful perusal. . . . The whole question is one of the greatest importance at the present moment. . . . The pity is that Parliament cannot spare time for a consideration of a reform that lies so nearly at the root of the happiness and welfare of the people. Mr. Rider Haggard's Report will do good if it directs attention to a subject which is of national and imperial interest.

It is very likely that the Report presented by Mr. Rider Haggard upon the question of the settlement of communities on land in our Colonies will lead to an important movement, affecting at the same time both the question of colonisation and the unemployed problem.

The Nottingham Guardian.—The Colonial Secretary formed the bold and original idea that it might be possible to dispose of some of our surplus unemployed in the British Colonies. So far as Mr. Rider Haggard's experience goes it is decidedly favourable to the scheme, and as he certainly knows what he is talking about when he deals with agricultural subjects, his opinion has weight.

The Western Morning News.—Mr. Rider Haggard's valuable Report on The Salvation Army Colonies must not be pigeon-holed and forgotten. It is also desirable that the investigation should be extended to South Africa. Sir John Gorst will next week inquire whether the Government propose to send a Commissioner to South Africa to inquire into the suitability of that country for land settlements. Mr. Haggard offered in his Report to investigate the possibility of setting up land colonies on similar lines and managed by the same machinery within the United Kingdom. That would be at least as practical as supplying the Colonies with bounty-fed settlers, and it is hoped that his offer will be accepted. He is thoroughly acquainted with the conditions of rural life.

The Western Daily Mercury.—Members of Parliament, who are interested in the question of Labour Colonies and Settlements are anxious not to let the Government fall away from the fair promise that

has been given of some action in the direction of helping the establishment of such institutions as a means of dealing with the unemployed
problem. They are particularly desirous that the services of Mr. Rider
Haggard should be used as he suggested in his recent Report to prepare
a memorandum on the possibility of establishing Colonies in the
United Kingdom.

The Western Mail.—Now that the Colonial Conferences are so much
talked about why not make this subject of Imperial land settlements
a question for discussion, to see if all the Colonies and the Mother
Country in combination cannot arrive at some plan whereby the surplus
population of the British Empire can be distributed with advantage to
the whole? Of course, it must not be merely the dumping of the
vicious upon Colonial shores. That would be too much after the
fashion of the old penal settlements. There is, however, some of the
country's best bone and muscle running to waste in unemployment,
and from any assisted scheme of emigration and colonisation the
Empire, as a whole, would benefit.

The Bath Herald.—It is a large and generous scheme that Canada
offers for our unemployed—the ten townships running to 240,000 acres
is magnificent, still, not only is capital required for the start, but there
must be a careful selection of persons.

Bristol Evening News.—It is evident that Mr. Rider Haggard has
approached a difficult problem with a sincere desire to find a solution,
and, sooner or later, his Report must be followed by some action by
the Government. . . . The Report has appeared at a time when the
unemployed problem is forcing itself on the attention of politicians and
social reformers, and Mr. Rider Haggard's suggestions possess the
merit of being eminently practical.

Bristol Times.—If Mr. Rider Haggard were less of a practical
agriculturist than he is, we should be disposed to regard his Report on
The Salvation Army Farm Colonies as too sanguine in tone. . . . It
may be assumed that his survey of life and labour on The Salvation
Army Colonies was made with characteristic thoroughness, and that
his conclusions are something quite different from those of a mere
sentimental amateur. . . . Not only the indigent people of the rural
labourer type, but those who have long been dwellers amid the poverty
of town, can be transplanted back to the land and prosper . . . it is to
be remembered that, as matters are now, the congestion in our cities
entails, as this Report points out, not only " degradation and misery,"
but a growing burden of " expense to the public ".

The South Wales Daily News.—Here is an outlet for the unemployed,
and the possible solution—even if partial—of a great and pressing
problem. But, it seems to us, a good deal could be done at home.
" Back to the land " is the cry. Very well. Why not allow the tiller of
the soil to have a personal interest in it ? why not have small holdings
under such conditions that the labourer will not be driven to the towns
to swell the lists of the unemployed, and create the worst problems
that public men have to face? The Salvation Army has given an
excellent lead ; and Mr. Haggard's scheme recommends itself.

Bristol Evening Times.—With the details of Mr. Haggard's study and emphatic approval of the Salvation Army's United States work we cannot deal now. But if they bear investigation, the Report goes far to make land settlement the most hopeful of social policies.

The Hull News.—A sensible scheme. The scheme, if properly managed, should prove a ready solution of the difficulty, not only of the "submerged tenth," but also, to some extent, of the unemployed question. . . .
Its objects are such that should command the sympathy and support of every agriculturist.

Grimsby Telegraph.—Were the State to take up the matter, however, and provide the necessary money, there is no doubt whatever that the result would be of immense benefit alike to the Empire and to the class immediately concerned.

Huddersfield Chronicle.—Generally speaking, his conclusions may be regarded as confidently affirmative, and in the main his proposals are eminently worthy of the most serious consideration, albeit some of them are by no means devoid of financial and economic difficulties. The Report is a very welcome one, and if it does not entirely solve the unemployed problem, it at least throws a good deal of light on it by indicating various methods by which the acuteness of the present situation in our great cities and towns may be relieved to at least some extent. . . . As we have said, the Report does not remove all the difficulties of the situation; but if the scheme is adopted, even partially at first, it should prove the means of providing happy homes for a few thousands of those starving millions who now throng our cities.

The Folkestone Express.—The Report presented by Mr. Rider Haggard on his visit to the Farm Colonies of America, and his conference with the Government authorities in Canada has been discussed with great interest. As soon as Parliament has time to attend to it, the subject of transplanting workers in congested districts of the old country to the spacious Colonies is sure to be taken up. Mr. Haggard gives numberless instances of the benefits conferred on British workers who were in hopeless poverty at home by placing them in positions in Canada where they are on the high road to comparative wealth. From the economic point of view, this transplantation of British citizens is a sound idea, and from the point of view of imperialism, it appeals to the imagination even more forcibly than schemes of Tariff Reform.

Nottingham Evening Post.—That the Salvation Army's Labour Colonies in America have borne the scrutiny of such a practical man as Mr. Rider Haggard is highly creditable to the sagacity and enterprise of their founders. His Report will do much to encourage schemes for getting the people back to the land, both in this country and abroad. Not the least satisfactory feature of it is the testimony it gives as to the possibility of teaching even townsfolk to become good farmers.

The Scotsman (Edinburgh).—Every practical and well-considered suggestion for the solution or mitigation of that burning social problem, the depopulation of the rural districts and the congestion of urban areas, deserves careful and respectful consideration. Mr. Haggard has special claims to be heard upon a question to which he has given close and earnest thought.

The Glasgow Herald.—As a missionary of Empire, Mr. Haggard must be credited with the capacity of thinking Imperially.

The Glasgow Evening News.—Mr. Rider Haggard's Report on The Salvation Army Colonies in the United States and in England is an admirably sane and lucid, and, on the whole, extremely encouraging document. . . . His report is of particular value at this time, when the "unemployed" problem is so seriously pressing for attention, and it is to be hoped it will receive the consideration it deserves.

The Aberdeen Journal.—The Report which Mr. Rider Haggard has furnished the Colonial Office on a scheme for land settlement is a document at once of great and interesting importance. . . . His view of The Salvation Army Colonies is an entirely favourable one, and he is very strongly in favour of the Imperial Government taking a similar scheme in hand with a view to relieving the congestion in towns and slums and getting the population back to the land. . . .

The Aberdeen Evening Gazette.—Mr. Rider Haggard's Report on the United States Colonies of the Salvation Army is of such importance, his proposals are so bold, and his praise of the work of The Army is so unqualified, that a desire is naturally created to know more of the guiding principles and inner workings of the Settlements referred to. In their objects and methods of working these Colonies are unique— they are unlike any other labour or farm colonies. . . .

The Dundee Courier.—Mr. Rider Haggard's visit to the United States in the beginning of the year is likely to have a practical and very desirable outcome. . . . But, important as the scheme is in its possibilities of giving to the unfortunate an opportunity of shaping a career for themselves, its Imperial aspect is hardly less striking. It is desirable that, as far as possible, emigrants from our shores should find a home within the bounds of the Empire instead of becoming subjects under another flag. The readiness with which Canada has shown her practical patriotism in offering to provide 240,000 acres as a start for the proposed Imperial settlements is very gratifying, and we do not doubt others of our Colonies who can furnish the land will follow her good example.

The Dundee Advertiser.—In his Report to the Colonial Office on the Salvation Army Farm Colonies, Mr. Rider Haggard pays that body a high compliment, and if his recommendations are adopted it will find itself in a unique position. . . . A scheme carried out entirely by Government officials would, Mr. Haggard believes, break down here, and he is right. That in its existing Colonies the Salvation Army has chosen just the right people is rare testimony to the thoroughness of its work and the minuteness of its officers' acquaintance with the character and potentialities of the people among whom they labour.

The Northern Whig.—Those who have studied that most difficult of present-day problems for those who wish to work will turn with interest to Mr. Rider Haggard's Report. . . . With so much land uncultivated at home, and large tracts abroad, there is no reason why any person who is willing and able to work should suffer from hunger. Mr. Haggard's Report opens up a wide vista for those who are striving to repair the damage done by poverty. In the interests of the ratepayers, as much as the poor, it is to be hoped that something practical will be done.

Labour Leader.—When Mr. Rider Haggard goes on to suggest that he hopes he may be allowed to prepare a separate memorandum on the possibility of establishment of rural Colonies in the United Kingdom under the same machinery to be used for the over-sea Colonies, we are with him. The cure for the unemployment should begin at home, where the evil has been generated.

THE ABERDEEN UNIVERSITY PRESS LIMITED

www.ingramcontent.com/pod-product-compliance
Lightning Source LLC
Chambersburg PA
CBHW030521100426
42813CB00001B/111